Love, Guaranteed

LOVE,
GUARANTEED!

How Husbands and Wives
Grow and Stay Together

DR. KEN TUCKER
AND JUDY TUCKER

NASHVILLE

NEW YORK • LONDON • MELBOURNE • VANCOUVER

Love Guaranteed

How Husbands and Wives Grow and Stay Together

Published in New York, New York, by Morgan James Publishing. Morgan James is a trademark of Morgan James, LLC. www.MorganJamesPublishing.com

Proudly distributed by Publishers Group West®

All Scripture quotations are from The ESV Bible, *The Holy Bible,* English Standard Version (ESV) Copyright 2001 by Crossway, a publishing ministry of Good News Publishers. Used by permission. All rights reserved.

Proverbs 5:15-18 Scripture taken from AMPLIFIED BIBLE, Copyright 1954, 1958, 1962, 1964, 1965, 1987 by The Lockman Foundation. All rights reserved. Used by permission. Parentheses are author's comments.

 Morgan James BOGO™

A **FREE** ebook edition is available for you or a friend with the purchase of this print book.

CLEARLY SIGN YOUR NAME ABOVE

Instructions to claim your free ebook edition:
1. Visit MorganJamesBOGO.com
2. Sign your name CLEARLY in the space above
3. Complete the form and submit a photo of this entire page
4. You or your friend can download the ebook to your preferred device

ISBN 9781636981925 paperback
ISBN 9781636981932 ebook
Library of Congress Control Number: 2023937088

Cover Design by:
Rachel Lopez
www.r2cdesign.com

Interior Design by:
Christopher Kirk
www.GFSstudio.com

Morgan James is a proud partner of Habitat for Humanity Peninsula and Greater Williamsburg. Partners in building since 2006.

Get involved today! Visit: www.morgan-james-publishing.com/giving-back

For our children, Kendra and Tony, Kristen, Kenny and Lizzy; our granddaughters, Madelyn and Layah; our grandsons, James Montgomery and Austin, and countless other offspring, those couples we have been blessed to serve, you are all the beneficiaries of us coming to accept from God and giving to each other love, guaranteed.

Table of Contents

Appendix

Acknowledgments

I want to thank my accountability partners, Van Brown, Gil Maycock, and Kersch Darville, for their gentle, at times firm counsel, guidance, and encouragement throughout the decades of staying with me through my difficult and transformative journey. Thank you, Dr. John Trent and Dr. Scott Harris for your thoughtful leadership, wisdom, mentorship, and belief in me. Thank you also to all my professors both in my master's and doctoral programs at Dallas Theological Seminary for your inspiration, challenge, and faithfulness to the Word of God.

Throughout the several years of sitting under your tutelage, the Holy Spirit has used each of you to guide me in life, to grow and refine me and help me conform to his likeness. I am eternally grateful to each of these individuals.

I want to especially thank my editor, Jenae Edwards, whose untiring devotion to God's Truth and excellence in writing has refined and polished my raw thoughts into articulate and clear lessons for husbands and wives to follow.

Finally, I want to thank my precious wife, Judy, my co-author and life partner. This book captures the story of His amazing grace in your life and serves as a testimony of your obedience to our Savior. Thank you for your faithfulness, diligence, sacrificial love, and unwavering commitment to me. I cannot imagine my life without you.

Foreword

We live in such a chaotic, changing, challenging world that the very idea of putting a "guarantee" on love may seem impossible. But before you throw up your hands or close this book, let Dr. Ken Tucker and his wife, Judy, share and show you something hugely important to your marriage—how despite all the challenges all marriages face in the chaos and brokenness of our world, the committed, changeless love God can bring into your home really can cause your marriage to grow and thrive.

As you meet Dr. Ken and Judy through this book, you'll find you're not just being handed a map. You have embarked on a journey with two world-class guides to help you. A couple who has been there. Done that. Driven the streets. Dealt with the challenges. They know the great places to go—and the places to avoid at all costs.

In short, you're about to find hands-on-help from a couple who have spent years doing life together well through great times and great challenges. They are living out, studying, and researching how to both build—and *rebuild* if needed—a strong, loving, lasting marriage.

Get ready to create and frame a new picture of your home—one full of help and hope. No dishing out shame for being imperfect here. Rather Ken and Judy share what they've learned from experience about holding fast to God's love—and loving like Jesus. His love lies at the heart of what *really can* make love last—and even reverse the curse for us if we come from a difficult background.

Over the next twelve chapters, you'll gain wisdom for how to face the challenges of culture and unpack the realities of what romance really is and can be. You will find, in Scripture and Ken and Judy's story, take-home-now ways to grow closer than you may have seen or dreamed.

Dr. Ken and Judy Tucker have a way of writing that will draw you in from chapter to chapter—from where you are now to the place and person you want to be and need to become for yourself, for your spouse, for your children, and for your God.

John Trent, Ph.D.

President, StrongFamilies.com the Center
    for StrongFamilies
Author of *"Where do I go from here?"* and
    Co-Author of *The Blessing*

CHAPTER I

"Not Loving" Rather than Loving

I am the man identified and discussed in the following chapters. I am the man, who like you, is a product of his environment, experiences, and choices. My culture has molded and shaped me. I mimic my primary caregivers' behavior and their understanding of love. Every topic, every challenge, every lesson, every good and bad decision, each failure and every sin, every confession and repentant act come from experiences in my life and marriage.

This book is for husbands who desire to love God more and who want to know how to love their wives better. This is also for wives who want to know how they can help their husbands love more deeply. Alongside funny stories, there will be calls to repentance when we will have the opportunity to confess and own up to our failures. There will be moments of celebration for our successes. This book reminds us of what God has done and is doing in and through those who are willing to yield control to him.

The stereotype for men is that they are emotionally and relationally clueless, but our culture does not tell the whole story. It is not your fault for failing to know how to love well. The fault lies in who taught us how to love. Who was your role model, and how did he set the expectation for how you should love?

Most likely your father or some other husband modeled what a loving husband should look like. What was that like for you? How did they show love? Based on the divorce rate and the frequency of husbands' infidelities, I would suggest that men who modeled what it means to be a loving husband might have been few or non-existent in your childhood. You are not to blame for not knowing how to love. Husbands were 'not loving' long before our generation. Unfortunately, our fathers passed on to us the distorted version of love that they received from their fathers, whose fathers also instilled a warped picture of love in them.

Within every family, a standard and demonstration of love is handed down from generation to generation. For example, the Pew Research Center reports that 63 percent of previously married people aged 45–54 will remarry; 67 percent of those previously married, age 55–64 will remarry; from age 65 up, 50 percent will remarry. These percentages suggest the last three generations are less likely to have seen a model of resilient, durable, and long-lasting love. Instead, you or your spouse are likely to have witnessed parents who at one time loved one another but are now divorced.

If you are twenty-five years or younger, you or your spouse are likely from a blended family: one in which siblings have only one parent in common. This means that one parent or the other loved someone else enough in the past to want to build a family with them but lost that kind of love for the other person. It is reasonable to conclude that past generations and present-day spouses, based on the high rate of divorce and remarriage, are either confused about what it takes, do not care enough, or do not know how to remain in a love relationship with the same spouse for a lifetime. Fellow husbands, we did not distort love; we are suffering from and perpetuating an inherited, perverted view of what love is.

In November 1984, Mick Jones wrote the song, "I Wanna Know What Love is," which not only captures the sentiments of his generation but accurately forecasts the longing of the present. These words echo an ongoing and compelling human need—one that bubbles up and spills out into song. Jones explains how this song came to be: "I always worked late at night, when everybody left, and the phone stopped ringing. 'I Want to Know What Love Is' came up at three in the morning sometime in 1984. I don't know where it came from. I consider it a gift that was sent through me. I think there was something bigger than me behind it. I'd say it was probably written entirely by a higher force."[1] Though Mick does not know where his lyrics came from, as Christians, we know the source of this longing. God created the appetite to love and be loved in us. He made mankind with the desire and need to know love. And knowing God is the only way to experience pure and perfect love. God is love, and only His love is complete and unfailing. Humans, on the other hand, love imperfectly.

Though we yearn to know what love is, we are not getting any better at it. In our marriages, husbands are not getting any better at continuously and faithfully loving our wives. In this way, we too are full-fledged participants in what has gone awry. Husbands play a key role and are responsible for how future generations of husbands love their wives. If you are a husband, you are by default a role model of either how to love or how not to love.

Growing up, I had several men model how NOT to love your wife. The problem is I did not realize they were teaching me how not to love. In fact, the husbands who influenced me did not know they were demonstrating how to be 'not loving.' They thought they were loving their wives. Some did not realize that being a hard worker and good provider or giving expensive gifts did not define loving their wife, particularly if they were doing the same for another woman at the same time.

Other husbands exemplified a more subtle form of 'not loving.' These men had legitimate hobbies—golf, football, video games or hanging out regularly with their boys. The problem was their wives came a distant second to their favorite past-time. She got what was left after everything else. Some husbands' 'not love' showed up in their domineering control or in their derogatory and demeaning way of treating their wives. It is easy not to love as a husband because it is our natural tendency. All husbands generally and instinctively default to 'not loving.' If left to their own devices, they become adulterous, emotionally absent, or domineering.

This was the case in Ephesus during the first century. Jewish husbands were socialized to see wives as just a little higher than servants. Greek husbands had an even lower opinion of their spouses. Demosthenes, a Greek philosopher and orator, reveals the general sentiment of husbands in his day: "We have courtesans for the sake of pleasure, we have concubines for the sake of daily cohabitation, and we have wives for the purpose of having children legitimately and being faithful guardians for our household affairs."[2]

As Demosthenes describes above, wives in first-century Asia Minor were seen as convenient tools that made them legitimate. Hence, Paul's instructions to husbands "to love their wives" in his letter to the Ephesian Christians was loaded with cultural and spiritual ramifications. In this one command, he denounces the cultural norms of his day. For instance, for the Romans, it was customary for husbands to find their sexual satisfaction with concubines and prostitutes. They also encouraged and expected their wives to likewise get their gratification from someone outside of their marriage, including household slaves.

Second, Paul in this letter, establishes marital parameters for the Christian husband. They are to love their wives singularly and devotedly. Instead of seeking self-gratification in a sinful promiscuous way, they are to instead love in a self-sacrificing way. Unbelieving husbands, according to societal norms, may 'not love' their wives, but Christian husbands must in a countercultural way do the remarkable—they must love their wives with a holy love.

Holy Love is Noticeably Uncommon

What does this kind of love look like? How can human husbands love like God, who Himself is love? This book discusses these questions and others. Here is an overview of what each chapter contains. This chapter explains how societies generationally set a standard for what is considered acceptable behavior. These behaviors and practices are more likely 'not loving' rather than loving. Chapter 2 walks through a survey of wives which concludes that they generally feel love is missing from their marriages. Though the husband is supposed to be the fountainhead of love in his family, this is not the case. Therefore, in this chapter, we will explain how every husband can learn to practice romance God's way. Chapter 3 describes how romance God's way looks—it is giving rather than getting. Chapter 4 highlights how romance God's way includes leaving, cleaving, and pursuing. Chapter 5 introduces attachment theory and how it aligns with the great separation that occurred in Genesis 3. Here, we also discuss the gracious reconnection to God, which empowers us to love like Christ. In this chapter, my wife Judy and I share how the Lord redeemed our marriage. We go deeper into our marriage story and how God pursued us in chapter 6. Chapters 7 through 12 provide specific applications for how to romance your wife based on 1 Corinthians 13:4–8:

Chapter 7: Love is patient rather than self-gratifying.
Chapter 8: Love is kind rather than unkind.
Chapter 9: Love promotes Truth rather than self.
Chapter 10: Love steps up rather than backs down.
Chapter 11: Love is permanent rather than transient.
Chapter 12: Reimagine loving rather than 'not loving.'

CHAPTER 2

Absent
Rather than Abundant

Some time ago, my wife, Judy, and I, were dining in Harpers Ferry, West Virginia when an attendant made an impression upon both of us that we have never forgotten. It had nothing to do with the service or even the conversation we had with her. We were indelibly impacted by what she had tattooed on her collarbone. Perfectly centered slightly above the neckline of her blouse was written the words, "Love is missing." We asked her what it meant. She responded politely, then definitively ended the conversation. But she did not stop the spiral of questions in my head: What provoked her to tattoo those words on her skin? What experiences did those words capture? Did she have a happy childhood? Was she now leading a satisfying life?

Sadly, as Judy and I counsel couples, they may as well have "Love is missing" tattooed on their neckline too. For many spouses, love is missing in their marriages. But this is not the way it should be. The Bible specifically commands husbands to ensure that love is abundant in their marriages. Ephesians 5: 25 commands, "Husbands, love your wives, as Christ loved the church and gave himself up for her." Wives are not given this directive. Husbands are specifically commanded to be the standard bearer of love in their marriage; they are to love their brides like Jesus loves his.

Jesus lavishes love upon His bride, and his example of love sets the standard for husbands to follow. The wording in Ephesians is emphatic: to be a Christian husband, one must love like Christ. To love like Christ is to demonstrate the greatest kind of love—where one lays down their life for another (John 15:13). I confess my failure in this regard. For far too long, I languished in a state of resentment and anger instead of lovingly caring for my wife. Too often, my love was stingy rather than lavish, conditional rather than compassionate, selfish rather than sacrificial. I loved me above loving her.

You might not feel the same way. You may feel you are loving your wife the best way you know how. You are faithful; you work hard to provide for your family; you even help with household chores. You remember her birthday and your anniversary, and you never forget to give chocolate and flowers on Valentine's Day. As a husband you may say, "I'm good. I am doing just fine." But go ask your wife. Ask her if you love her so well, so unfailingly, that you do not need to read a book like this.

We did ask wives—maybe not yours specifically—but we asked a group of 100 wives from different backgrounds, who had been married from 1 to 55 years, to rate how they felt about the love they were receiving from their husbands. They responded on a scale from 1 to 5 where "5" was, "I am absolutely fulfilled by the love I am getting from my husband;" and "1" was, "I am absolutely starving and hurting from lack of love from my husband." Here are the results of the study:

- 20 percent responded, "5."
- 35 percent responded, "4."
- 20 percent responded, "3."
- 5 percent responded, "2."
- 20 percent responded, "1."

Eighty percent of the wives' responses in our survey suggested that husbands were falling short of loving in a way that was completely satisfying to them.

This is not the way it is supposed to be. Christian husbands are called and should be equipped to demonstrate God's kind of love. We are to be God's standard for other men—examples of what love can really look like in marriage—as husbands who mimic Christ's self-sacrificial love. Our wives know painfully well that we are falling short of our calling. They long to see us step up and model a higher standard of love in our homes. Unfortunately, many husbands fail to be the nourishing resources of love in their marriages. Instead of being the conduit, the means through which life-giving love flows, we might be a sickness that eats away at and eventually kills the healthy cells of love in our marriage. At least I was.

In my marriage with Judy, I was a cancerous sore tearing away at the faith, love, and commitment Judy was working hard to maintain. I struggled to understand why I did what I did. What was at the root of my devastating behavior? I realize now that my questions were the Holy Spirit convicting me of my sin. I wrestled with His conviction for years until I came to understand what I now know to be true of me and what I believe may be true for many unfaithful husbands. Love was missing.

I do not mean that love is missing from our wives toward us. For many of us, the genuine and enduring love of our wives is the one thing keeping us from suicidal hopelessness. Judy's love for God and her lovingness toward me eventually brought me back to God and back to loving her. My return to God and Judy began when I owned and accepted that my behavior was evidence that love was missing. How I lived and what I practiced clearly showed that I did not possess love. I said I loved, but I did not 'do' love. Love was missing from my thinking. I had no concept of what it meant to love genuinely, much less what it meant to love sacrificially. This discovery was my first step towards intimacy with my Lord and my wife. In this same way, for many Christian men, love is missing. Since love is missing for them, maybe even foreign to them, it is likewise missing in their relationship with their wives.

After living a lukewarm Christian life for most of my marriage, I started wrestling with what it means to love God and how that might impact the way I love my wife. This book explains how Scripture teaches husbands to love God and their wives, and it also explains how these two loves are inseparable. Rightly loving God leads to rightly loving my wife. Rightly loving my wife is the only way I can be right with God.

For the Christian husband, anything less than daily sacrificial love towards his wife represents disobedience and failure. It is disobedience not to love our wives like Christ unconditionally loves his church. It is failure on our part when we give our wives reasons to doubt our love. Paul in Ephesians 4:1, guided by the Holy Spirit, commands the saints to walk worthy of their calling. For the Christian husband, walking worthy involves three behaviors: loving your wife like Christ loves the Church (Ephesians 5:25), loving your wife in a way that helps her to grow in holiness (5:27), and loving your wife like your own body (5:28).

This is some heavy love—too heavy in fact for any human husband to carry on his own. We need a new way of thinking to love like Christ. Our present way of thinking about marriage is distorted, and our capacity to love is deficient. However, hope is found in God's Word. The Bible is clear about what went and what goes wrong in marriage. It provides specific remedies for hurting couples and faltering husbands, and Scripture gives clear examples of what renewed thinking about marriage looks like.

What Makes Loving So Hard?

Why is loving our wives such a problem to begin with? Why do we not naturally love the women who in most instances are already loving us? The simple and biblical answer is, there is something wrong with our thinking. Something is wrong with our hearts (Jeremiah 17:9–

10). "Thinking" is often described using the analogy of the condition of our hearts. We inherit a defective heart. Jeremiah describes the heart as "deceitful above all things and desperately wicked." Since Adam, our thoughts have been bent towards evil, and our hearts are prone to sin (Romans 3:23).

Hence, wrong thinking about our wives started back when Adam sinned. The moment he ate of the Tree of the Knowledge of Good and Evil, Adam's perspective about God, himself, and Eve was permanently altered. Before his thinking was infected by sin, Adam saw Eve as what he longed for and needed to complete him. He articulated this in Genesis 2:23, "This at last is bone of my bones and flesh of my flesh; she shall be called Woman, because she was taken out of Man." He loved her deeply.

However, once Adam sinned, once his heart hardened, his thinking about her and thus his affection toward her changed from loving adoration to glaring accusation. He said, "The woman whom you gave to be with me, she gave me fruit of the tree, and I ate." These words are dismissive, demeaning, and derogative. Adam's change of thinking about Eve, and subsequently, every husband's innate negative thinking toward their wives has cascaded into the human race. At the same time, because of Eve, the wives' innate thinking about their husbands was indelibly impacted as well. God explains how wives' thinking towards their husbands was altered because of the Fall. He said to Eve, "Your desire shall be contrary to your husband, but he shall rule over you" (Genesis 3:16).

Thus, after the Fall, wives would never again be easy to love. The sin nature in women will turn them against their husbands causing them to strive to control them—to usurp their leadership role. Two previously perfect beings originally joined together in complete harmony became two sinners juxtaposed to each other in unending tension and conflict because of sin. Adam and all husbands that follow him are inclined to resent and blame their wives. Eve and wives thereafter, because of sin, are inclined to disrespect and resist their husbands' leadership.

Hence, our rebellion in the Garden distorted and derailed our mindset and mental framework about marriage from what it was supposed to be. So how do we fix it? How do we reverse the damage that Adam and Eve initiated? Genesis has the answer.

In Genesis, the book of beginnings, the process of creating man is punctuated in a way that sets this act apart from all the other things God created. The rhythm in Genesis 1 is, and God said, "Let there be . . . ," and whatever He said came into being. He said, let there be light, and there was light; let there be an expanse in the midst of the waters, and it was so; let there be living creatures in the sea, and they appeared, and so on. But, in Genesis 1:26, the cadence of "God said. . . and there was" is interrupted. It is as if God took a reflective pause in his creative process to emphasize this pivotal event.

Instead of speaking to the elements as He had done previously, God began to speak to Himself: "And God said, 'Let us make man in our image, after our likeness.'" At this point, God intensified His involvement in Creation. In comparison, He created much of the world remotely but not so with His premier creation. For this act, God got down into the dirt. God did not speak man into being, ". . . the Lord God formed man of the dust from the ground . . ." (Genesis 2:7). He made man in a special way to be special in Creation. Only humans were made in God's image. Only man was given dominion over "every living thing" (Genesis 1:28).

Man was given dignity and value like no other part of Creation. And he was positioned with authority as God's sub-regent—His representative on earth. He made them male and female to fully image Him. The human male and female, together, are the full expression of the image of God. Adam alone cannot completely image the Triune God, for God is relational by nature. He exists in community with Himself. God the Father, Son, and Holy Spirit exist in perfect harmony. They are intimately engaged in a never-ending, always happening relationship. He made Adam and Eve to reflect this permanency as they too were to live in an intimate unending relationship with one another.

This triad—the husband and wife walking with God and living in holy intimacy—is illustrative of the oneness that exists between the Father, Son, and Holy Ghost. He also designed mankind so that they could and would produce other image bearers—others who would walk with God.

To be the *imago dei*—to faithfully represent Him—is the chief purpose for which He made man and woman, albeit the Fall distorted the display and manifestation of the image of God. However, the command, purpose, and reality of being His image remains. God's undeterred plan is that we image Him in the world at large and in marriage in particular.

This is the premise upon which a God-centered marriage and family is built. Adam and Eve as husband and wife were the perfect icon of the presence of God amongst His creation. In the same way, a Christian husband and wife walking in oneness can be examples of fully functioning image bearers. Ideally, as each spouse obediently walks with God, they can be a billboard—a display of how marriage glorifies God.

We exist for His glory. We were created to spread His fame. The problem is, as mentioned above, our ability to function fully as His image has been marred and distorted by sin. As a result, marriage is now the coming together of two sinners—a fusion of two dysfunctional image bearers. However, Christ came and provided the means by which we may re-connect to God and become more fully functioning as His representatives on earth and in our marriages.

A husband's demonstrated love for his wife and a wife's willing respect for her husband are together a model of how to love for the next generation. In this way, marriage is ideally a love-manufacturing, love-modelling opportunity. After all, God determined that "it was not good for man to be alone" (Gen 2:18). He identified that Adam needed someone to love and someone to love him. He designed Adam and Eve's body to come together in the love-making act to reproduce baby image bearers.

Doing this, God determined and designed them as *vehicles* through which He would transmit generations of loving image bearers, who, like Adam and Eve, would continue in perfect God-to-human, human-to-God, human-to-human relationships. Alas, Adam and Eve rebelled against God's design and by doing so imputed to us death and separation from God.

By their act of disobedience, their relationship with God and each other was perverted. Consequently, marriage and the family are no longer the way they are supposed to be. We live a distorted and limited version of God's original design for husbands and wives. We were created to have dominion over everything (Gen 1:28), but instead, we are now enslaved to evil desires and depravity.

However, despite man's sinful condition, we are still God's idea. We are still His creation, and though depraved and dead in sin, we are still His image. As image-bearers, we have a sense of and the instinct to pursue purpose. That purpose is still to reflect Him in the world. I believe all humans sense that purpose—that life is more than what we see. We instinctively wonder or suspect that there is more to us than the tangible. It is that invisible, non-tangible, mysterious aspect to life that we refer to as that which is "spiritual." We recognize its existence, and we yearn to know it. God designed us so. We are born with an innate need that drives us to pursue the spiritual.

This yearning to grasp ahold of that which is spiritual is so compelling that it is best described as a quest. Humans are on a quest: we *desire* a life that is spiritual. This craving for something more, to be "spiritual," is naturally elusive and mysterious to us.

For Christians, however, the quest is clear and personally realized. By God's grace and salvation, we have a restored relationship with Him, and because of that we are called to a renewed way of thinking about marriage. Men do not have to be bad husbands like our predecessors. Because of His Spirit within us, we are no longer prisoners to Adam's nature. We can experience restoration, which removes separation between us and God. When we repent and turn from our sin, we release God's power to make us into the men he would have us to be. By this, we are empowered to move towards his ultimate plan of oneness—becoming one with him and with our spouse.

Subsequently, Christian husbands must work to fulfill the urgent mission to image Christ in our marriages: to love like Him, to serve like Him, and to live as Him in our marriages. This is the gender-specific mandate He is calling Christian husbands to own. The man in a marriage is ordained and charged by God with creating an environment of love in their homes to help their wives grow up in the Lord (Ephesians 5:28). However, for this to happen, we need an extreme makeover of how we think about marriage and how we imagine our roles as lovers.

We Inherit a Perverted Love Mindset from Our Family and Culture

The pure thinking and perfect state the first couple had in Eden is gone. The sinful and sensual influences of sexually infused movies, explicit web sites, tantalizing TV commercials, casual hook ups, and Tinder one-night stands are abundant. This is not the way it is supposed to be, nor is it the way it should or could be for Christian households. Christian husbands, we are called to set a holy standard. We are called to proclaim and practice as Joshua modeled, "As for me and my house we will serve the Lord" (Joshua 24:15). We are called to have the mindset of David as he repented of his adultery in Psalm 51: "Have mercy on me, O God, according to your steadfast love; according to your abundant mercy blot out my transgressions. Wash me thoroughly from my iniquity and cleanse me from my sin! For I know my transgressions, and my sin is ever before me."

To help us live like this in our marriages, Scripture provides the context and instruction for how we should reframe our thinking, revamp our loving, and reinvigorate our passion for our wives. Ultimately, changing the way we love our wives requires changing the way we think about our relationship with God.

CHAPTER 3

Getting
Rather than Giving

Do you love your wife enough to give up your life for her? Many husbands would reply, "Yes" without hesitation. With sincerity and intent, most men see themselves as doing the grand deeds of stepping in front of a train, fighting off a charging lion, or taking a bullet for their wives. However, the smaller, non-life threatening, daily, sacrificial behavior is where husbands fail. For example, when my wife and I are in a marriage counseling session where the husband is the admitted offending party, we often ask, "Do you love your wife enough to give up alcohol? Do you love her enough to give up pornography? Do you love her enough to stop drinking in other women? Do you love her enough to look toward the other side of the road instead of at the jogging female?" The unspoken, expected answer is usually, "Yes."

However, reality sets in when we follow-up with this question: "So, why don't you? Why don't you give up the behaviors that are hurting your wife and destroying your marriage and testimony?"

Husband, what do you still have to give up to truly love your wife? What would it take? Ultimately, as suggested in the last chapter, a change in thinking that directs our hearts towards our wives is desperately needed. To do that, we must first deal with the thinking that leads us to misbehave by seeking to get rather than to give. Research reveals that many husbands are overcome with fleshly thinking that pulls them away from giving love to their wives. We are consumed by feeding and satisfying our carnal desires instead of loving our wives.

For example, a non-profit organization called Proven Men Ministries commissioned a 2014 survey conducted by Barna Group. This survey was given to a nationally represented sample of 388 self-identified,

Christian adult men. The statistics for Christian men between 18 and 30 years old are particularly striking:

- 77 percent looked at pornography at least monthly.
- 36 percent viewed pornography daily.
- 32 percent admitted being addicted to pornography (and another 12 percent thought they may be).

The statistics for middle-aged Christian men (ages 31 to 49) are no less disturbing:

- 77 percent looked at pornography while at work in the past three months.
- 64 percent viewed pornography at least monthly.
- 18 percent admitted being addicted to pornography (and another 8 percent thought they may be).

Even married Christian men are falling prey to pornography and extramarital sexual affairs at alarming rates:

- 55 percent looked at pornography at least monthly.
- 35 percent had an extramarital sexual affair.

These statistics confirm what we already know: there is a problem with pornography and affairs among Christian men. We are consumed with self-gratification. Men are in hot pursuit of the wrong thing. If you have ever struggled or are presently struggling with pornography or are wrestling with straying eyes or festering cold-heartedness towards your wife, this book is for you.

Romance is God's Idea

As mentioned in the last chapter, God designed Adam and Eve to produce other image bearers. To do this, He gave them an appetite for a specific activity—an intimate and euphoric fusion of two people's bodies, souls, and minds. He designed the man and the woman to desire one another. The man's desire is demonstrated most often in pursuit, and the woman's most often is expressed in being available and enamored by the pursuit. This emotional, arousing, and captivating dance is what we call romance.

When we are introduced to romance in the Book of Genesis, we come upon a scene where a man and woman are naked with one another. They are placed in a beautiful garden filled with a variety of fruit trees. Not a cloud can be seen in the sky. Birds are singing; bunnies are frolicking nearby; a pride of lions are looking on disinterested. Echoing in the background is the soothing sound of rushing water. As we draw closer to this couple, we get a whiff of the sweet-smelling air of newness. Their relationship is new. Their environment is new. Their love is new. Everything is perfect. This is almost heaven, and the narrator reveals in the very last verse of Genesis 2: ". . . the man and his wife were both naked and were not ashamed."

A movie's opening scene with a naked man and woman now would have a different plot than the one we see here in the Bible. But this was a God-designed, God-created event—this was romance God's way. Unfortunately, most of us have been exposed to Hollywood's version of romance. It is one of the influencers fueling sexual misconduct and sexual unfaithfulness in Christian marriages. But God created romance based on more than physical fulfillment. Romance in God's design encompasses the whole person while pleasing and glorifying Him.

Genesis helps us understand how God created romance—one that is built on obedience, serving, and pursuit. Genesis 2:18 states:

> Then the LORD God said, "It is not good that the man should be alone; I will make him a helper fit for him." Now out of the ground the LORD God had formed every beast of the field and every bird of the heavens and brought them to the man to see what he would call them. And whatever the man called every living creature, that was its name. The man gave names to all livestock and to the birds of the heavens

and to every beast of the field. But for Adam there was not found a helper fit for him. So, the LORD God caused a deep sleep to fall upon the man, and while he slept took one of his ribs and closed up its flesh. And the rib that the LORD God had taken from the man he made into a woman and brought her to the man. Then the man said, "This at last is bone of my bones and flesh of my flesh; she shall be called Woman, because she was taken out of Man." Therefore, a man shall leave his father and his mother and hold fast to his wife, and they shall become one flesh. And the man and his wife were both naked and were not ashamed.

In the first scene of this story, the first man meets the first woman, and they are joined together by the Almighty God. This is the moment when romance was written into human history, and God is the author of this couples' story (vs. 18). He wrote the script, designed the setting, developed the plot, and chose the characters. He made the man and the woman perfectly for each other. No other creature was a match. Adam declares, "This at last is bone of my bones and flesh of my flesh" (vs. 24). In saying this, Adam recognizes Eve as his perfect match. He expresses relief as if something has been lifted off him. We use the words "at last" when a delay has been endured, a gratification has been deferred. Adam says of Eve, "At last my waiting is over. At last, I have what I have been missing, what I have been lacking is now available to me. At last, I have it; at last, I see it; at last, I feel it; at last, I know it."

Timing is everything, and so it was with the sequence of events in the first human relationship. God created Adam first out of the dust in Genesis 2:7. He formed Eve later from one of Adam's ribs (vs. 21). Have you ever wondered why God did not simply make both Adam and Eve at the same time? Was Eve an afterthought? Was God so caught up in creating the universe, the planets, the sun, the moon, the stars, and man that he forgot that just like the lion would need a lioness and a tiger would need a tigress, man would need a woman? No, God's plan was to make them male and female all along (Genesis 1:26–27).

God did not mess up. He intentionally created man before woman. Why? The answer, I believe, is found in what Adam was doing before she came. I imagine Adam was learning three self-denying ways to love before Eve arrived. Adam was learning to love by obeying, by serving, and by pursuing.

Romance starts by obeying God. Jesus in John 14:15 affirms this durable principle, He says to his disciples then and now, "If you really love me, you will obey my commandments." This idea is repeated in 1 John 5:3, "For this is the love of God, that we keep his commandments." In other words, God's people show their love for Him by consistently obeying His commands. In Genesis 2:16–17, God sets Adam up to love his wife by giving him His Word to obey: "And the Lord God commanded the man, saying, 'You may surely eat of every tree of the Garden, but of the tree of the knowledge of good and evil you shall not eat, for in the day you eat of it you shall surely die.'"

God expects you, as a husband, to use the rational mind he gave you to do what is right. In giving this command to the newly-created-husband-to-be, God invited Adam to use his rational mind to tell the difference between right and wrong. Every husband can know right from wrong. We have guilt, and we have a sense of dread when we are doing something we know is wrong. Every person who looks at pornography knows at some level that it is wrong. This is why they do it in secret. Our God-given rational brain tells us there is something not quite right about what we are doing. Even the person who does not believe in God and has no knowledge of the Bible is still likely to conceal the fact that they are addicted to pornography.

God gave man a rational mind so that even though he was alone in the Garden, or for us today, alone in a hotel room, he may choose to love God by obeying Him. In the beginning, God gave Adam specific instructions by which to live: If you do this, you will live; If you do that, you will die. Obedience is submission—it is surrendering your will to the will of another. God requires that of us. Love motivates us to obey: "If anyone loves me, he will keep my word" (John 14:15). As we learn to surrender to God's thinking, it transforms ours. As we submit to Him, we become more like him. Every husband must do this first to love his wife at the high standard God sets for us.

In giving the command as to what he can and should not eat, God established Adam as a sentient being. Adam had all five senses. He could see, hear, smell, taste and feel, and God expected him to guard his heart against temptations that arose from his senses. As men, sight might be the most difficult sense to tame. God warns Adam to monitor, manage, and ignore his senses regarding one tree. Probably daily, walking by the center of the Garden, Adam could see and smell the fruit on the trees, including the alluring fruit on the Tree of the Knowledge of Good and Evil.

I imagine there were times when Adam felt like he deserved a treat. He had worked hard, and a little reward would be nice. Or maybe there were moments when the pressure was intense, and he longed for release. Or sometimes, he just wanted to try something new. I can imagine that at those times, the Tree of the Knowledge of Good and Evil in the middle of the Garden, reputed to have special powers, might have been even more tempting to him. But Adam did not give into his senses—at least not at first. He did not put his own pleasure above pleasing God. Although he lived alone, a state that God himself described as "not good for man," Adam was not the first to eat of the Tree of the Knowledge of Good and Evil. He could have, but he did not. Alone and lonely, Adam governed his senses rather than allowing them to rule him. Instead of seeking to take and eat what was forbidden, Adam used his time alone to give himself to God by obeying.

In giving Adam the "do not eat" instruction, God shows that he gave Adam the appetite to acquire and apply knowledge. Adam was able to learn by instruction and application. God equipped Adam with the ability to receive instruction—the ability to learn from what he was told in order to avoid making wrong choices. He also equipped Adam to learn from his mistakes—from going against God's Word and suffering the consequences.

In this context, as learning beings, we are inquisitive by God's design. God made Adam with an inquiring mind, which he used to figure out what an animal group should be called based on the distinguishing characteristics they possessed. God gives us the desire to explore and acquire information. Sadly, curiosity is one of the underlying drivers for the dismaying data I shared earlier: we are curious beings; we want to know; and we are intrigued to try new things. We all suffer from some fear of missing out. For far too many men, Adam included, this leads to devastating sin.

So, why did God give Adam such a compelling need to know? What was Adam supposed to do with it? God gave Adam and all humans inquisitiveness for the purpose of seeking after God: "The fear of the Lord is the beginning of wisdom. And the knowledge of the Holy One is understanding" (Proverbs 9:10). God's plan was, and is, for us to use our natural curiosity to know Him—to understand His purpose. Adam was freshly minted; he was a blank slate—a clean canvas. Everything around him was a new creation. There was so much he did not know and so much for him to learn. Everything God gave him, including the ability and curiosity to learn, he gave so that Adam may know Him, know himself, and understand others. This ability to know, to learn, and to make choices based on knowledge set Adam apart from all other animals. God gave man alone the capacity for intelligent choice.

LOVE IS MANIFESTED WHEN WE CHOOSE TO GIVE RATHER THAN TO GET.

In this context, the choice of whether to eat of the Tree of the Knowledge of Good and Evil was present every hour, every day. The Bible tells us it was pleasant to the eyes, good to the taste, and had the potential to impact ones' thinking. But Adam resisted; Adam chose to love, to give obedience to God rather than to satisfy himself. He did not eat the fruit. He did not disobey God by seeking *to get*. No, Adam chose *to give obedience* to honor God with his body and mind. We have the same choice and opportunity today. It is the choice between selfishly getting for ourselves or selflessly giving by seeking to know and obey His Word. Obedience to God, for husbands, is also demonstrated by actively pursuing our wives.

CHAPTER 4

Reprieve
Rather than Regret

A study in the year 2000 found that a husband is 218 percent more likely to cheat on his wife if he uses pornography than if he does not. Every adulterous act, all sexual misconduct, and every time we lust begins by focusing our minds upon pursuing someone, or something, other than our wives. Romancing our wives starts with learning how to love by obeying God's Word. Adam received this lesson. He knew which were the can-eat-and-enjoy-trees, and that they would bring a different result than the must-not-eat-shall-surely-die-tree. Romancing your wife has a different result than the devastation that comes with having sex with your computer or with someone in your mind.

Adam was created with a healthy, natural appetite. He had an appetite for food, for love, for companionship, and for romance. Adam was fully man; he apparently had the urges, wants, and needs that would lead him to eat. While waiting for Eve, for however long, God allowed Adam to learn to love by staying on course—to love by obeying. Psalms 119:9 asks, "How shall a young man keep himself sexually pure?" The answer is by conforming his ways and training his mind on the Word of God. Over and over Scripture uses phrases such as, "set your mind," "renew your mind," "let this mind," and "have this mind." All of these are active. We are to intentionally take control of our minds. In Genesis, we see God urging Adam, the first man, to use his mind in a way that is pleasing to God—to control his urges. I suggest that God was teaching Adam to have a God-centered mind.

Too often in matters of romance, we are not God-centered in our thinking. We see romance as sexual, but not spiritual; as human, not divine; as fleeting, not permanent; as self-gratifying, not God glorifying. Worse, we say we love God while resenting our wives (1 John 4:20).³ We tend to see pursuing God as distinct from pursuing our wives. But they are one in the same. If you are married today, you are not obeying God if you are not pursuing your wife. And likewise, you are failing your wife if you are not pursuing God. Pursuing God, having your mind set on Him, is the only way to love your wife like Christ loved the church.

Focusing your sexual, sensual, and intimate thoughts only upon your wife is the only way married men can be obedient to God. God was training the first man to focus his mind first and foremost on Him in order that he might be prepared to rightly lead and pursue his wife. To romance your wife, start by having a mind free from sexual sin. Train your mind in such a way so that all sensuous thoughts are holy before God and only about your wife. Romancing your wife is learning to love her by first obeying God. Are you obedient to God in your thought life today?

Romance is a Combination of Serving and Leading

Romance God's way is also about learning to serve by leading. And, consequently, learning to lead by serving. To romance your wife, you will need to learn how to lead her so that she experiences the love of Christ flowing through you to her. We can learn a lot about serving when we are the leader. For example, we learn to expect nothing in return. Leadership is a thankless job. People rarely think to say thanks for the sacrifices of time and effort it often requires to keep things running. We learn accountability. Even as we lead, we are held accountable by someone higher than us for what we accomplish.

Leaders learn that leading is about us being responsible for serving everybody else. This was the case for Adam in the Garden. Every time Adam named a new animal, he was reminded that he was alone. Each time he identified the unique characteristics of an animal, he realized once again that there was not another like him. Any time he noticed an animal curled up next to its mate, he remembered that he did not have a mate of his own. Scripture captures this sad commentary in Genesis 2:20: "The man gave names to all livestock and to the birds of the heavens and to every beast of the field. But for Adam there was not found a helper fit for him."

Adam was the solitary leader and servant in the Garden before Eve arrived. In my mind, this demonstrates how God views man. God sees man, the male, as the one he created first. He sees us as the ones he charged first with responsibility for his creation. He sees us as the one he holds accountable for the family. He sees the man as the one he holds responsible for modeling what it is like to be loved by him.

Ephesians 5:25, says, "Husbands love your wives as Christ loves the church." This is often read with a focus on marriage. And it should be. But it is also about the husband's leadership role in the home. To romance your wife is to lead her in such a way that she experiences the love of Christ flowing through you to her. We do not get to pawn off our leadership role to our wives.

God's design is for the man to be the leader in the home. His plan is for the wife to be her husband's partner in every other way. But you, husband, are responsible and accountable to God for leading your wife by serving her like Christ would. We are called to be the quintessential role model of Christ's love in our homes. Romancing your wife is to give up yourself for her, to serve her without the ulterior motive of expecting something in return.

To romance your wife is to lead by loving her like Christ loves the church. It is to lead self-sacrificially, and Adam led and served in the Garden in the following ways:

1. He was alone and naked before God: Let your wife see you bare and vulnerable before God.
2. He was busy and devoted to God: Let your wife observe you putting more emphasis on the things of God than on the things of earth.

3. He was willing to wait on God: Let your wife see your patience growing with her and with others.

4. He was enthusiastically receptive of the woman God gave him: Let your wife experience you celebrating her often.

Romancing your wife is learning to serve her by leading her to love Jesus more deeply. Romance God's way is learning to pursue your wife by yearning after her—in hot pursuit of her. God wants us to yearn after our wives. Even though Adam was quite busy learning and leading, he was also yearning. During your day at work, do you ever think about your woman? How much time are you feeding your mind with thoughts of loving on her? Amidst the activity in creation, this comment regarding Adam stands out, "But there was not found a helper fit for Adam." Adam felt it— he sensed something was missing. He may not have known exactly what was lacking, but he knew he did not have it. And it was not good.

God confirms that it was not good in Genesis 2:18, "It is not good that the man should be alone . . ." The funny thing is, it was not good for Adam because God made it so. The delay of God's creation of Eve was intentional. God meant for Adam to learn to control his desires. He instilled in Adam the desire for companionship and cohabitation. He put in Adam the desire for sexual union with one person for a lifetime. He did not design us to handle the memory of other sexual partners. In his plan, there is only one partner in our minds sexually—one person we have tasted and enjoyed and one person tasting and enjoying us.

Romance God's way flows from a husband to his wife only. Romance God's way is not to be spread thin over multiple partners over a lifetime but is to be given in rich full doses to one special person. The antidote to sexual deviance and misconduct is to spend each day in hot pursuit of your wife.

What Does Hot Pursuit Look Like?

Hot pursuit is how we can best understand and apply Genesis 2:24, "Therefore a man shall leave his father and his mother and hold fast to his wife." Two things in this verse speak specifically of pursuit. To "leave" speaks of a clean and abrupt break away from one's parents. God designed our desire to romance our wives, our yearning and pursuit after her to be so compelling that all other earthly affections fade in importance. Even our natural affinity to our parents is to be subjugated to our yearning and pursuit of our wives. To "cleave" means God designed romance to include two people and two people only: a man and woman as husband and wife. Proverbs 5:15–18 teaches:

Drink water from your own cistern (that of a pure marriage relationship). And fresh running water from your own well. Should your springs (your children) be dispersed, (with this baby momma or that one or that one over there) as streams of water in the streets? No, confine yourself to your own wife. Let your children be yours alone, and not the children of strangers with you. Let your fountain (your wife) be blessed with the rewards of your fidelity. And rejoice in the wife of your youth.

As taught in this passage, our relationship with our wives is to be one of a kind—isolated and off limits to all others. God intends for the husband to desire and pursue his wife only. This compelling pursuit is particularly evident in how Adam treated Eve after the Fall. How Adam interacted with his wife after sin entered the world is a very important lesson for all husbands. We live in post-Fall and post-Eden times. Like Adam after sin, we too are called to romance our wives in their fallen state while we ourselves are in our fallen state. Unlike pre-Fall when Adam was romancing a sinless woman with a pure mind and perfect understanding, Adam in Genesis 3 had to learn to romance and pursue a wife who was a sinner, having a mind himself that had been distorted by disobedience and darkened by sin. This, unfortunately, is our inherited situation and our depraved condition as husbands who are descendants of Adam.

The good news is romance God's way is still the same. The biblical principle of leaving and cleaving still applies, but not only that: along with "leave and cleave," "reprieve" was also introduced in the Garden.

Adam and Eve were condemned sinners. They went from a perfect relationship with God and each other to a broken one. Instantaneously, they went from harmony and happiness to horror and hopelessness. God immediately passed judgement on their sin and in his judgment, he provided a reprieve for Adam and Eve. Look at Genesis 3:21, "For the Lord God made for Adam and for his wife garments of skins and clothed them." In this act God pardoned them for their sin, he spilled blood and covered their nakedness and shame. Grace and mercy entered the world and their marriage.

The problem in Adam's marriage was insurmountable. He and his wife committed the most evil and egregious transgression against God and themselves of all time. Their selfish actions sentenced them and their offspring to death and eternal condemnation.

Initially, Adam blamed Eve for their problems. However, Genesis 4:1 illustrates how God can use a husband to reprieve and repair even the most devastating and hopeless of marriages: "Now Adam knew his wife Eve, and she conceived." This is not likely speaking of a one-time event but implies Adam's regular and recurring pursuit of romance toward his wife. Adam's heart did not stay hardened towards Eve. He returned to a tender romancing love for her. In doing this, Adam mimicked what God did for him and what God does for us. He gave grace and mercy to Eve. He reprieved his marriage from certain death.

Is your marriage dead or dying? Are your feelings dwindling or numb towards your spouse? Do you find it impossible to forgive or ask for forgiveness? Is there a third party, present and alluring—an interloper like the Serpent in your marriage? In confession and with regret, I have been there. However, just as Adam and Eve who by God's grace returned to oneness with one another despite adversity, God can use you or your spouse to restore and revamp your marriage.

God used my wife to reprieve me. I was done with my marriage, resentful towards my wife and far, far away from God. But God is faithful and so was Judy. To reap the full benefit of reprieve in my marriage, I had to actively pursue my wife. I had to come back to God, and he changed my heart towards my wife.

As a husband, you have already "left" your father and mother if you are married and no longer live in their house. You are at least partially *cleaving* to her if you are sharing the marriage bed and its pleasures. However, you are not *reprieving* if you are not intentionally romancing your wife and actively pursuing her. In Ephesians 5:25, the nature of *reprieve* is fueled by love that is quite remarkable and divine. Reprieve requires sacrifice; Christ provided the ultimate sacrifice. Reprieve requires esteeming the other person above ourselves; Christ humbled Himself to lift us up. Reprieve requires foregoing punishment; in Christ we are forgiven and no longer condemned. Reprieve requires loving the sinner; God loved us and sent Jesus to die for us even while we were still sinning. God reprieves perfectly, for it is his nature. He is love, and his love is steadfast and never ceases. Adam's love after the Fall, despite the Fall, was God-like—steadfast and merciful. He behaved like God in his marriage. He not only forgave the person who cost him everything, but he pursued her, just as Christ pursues his bride—with self-denying love.

How did Adam work through his disdain in Genesis 3—when he referred to Eve as "the woman"? Why did he stay in the marriage? Maybe he did not have another option? Regardless, due to the disdain Adam expressed earlier towards Eve, the absence of another romantic option would not have kept him at home. Disdain—contempt towards a spouse, is one of the four deadly horsemen known to lead to divorce according to Researcher John Gottman and others.[4] Contempt, they say, results in one partner assuming a position of moral superiority over the other. Adam said, "It is the woman. She did it. She ate the fruit." Contempt drives us to get away from the person—to withdraw from their presence. It does not necessarily create a need to go and be with someone else as much as it is a compelling desire to get away from *the source of disdain*. Many husbands find themselves in a situation such as Adam where an event leads them to develop disdain for their wife.

Some husbands, although they hold palpable disdain for their wives, feel rather proud of themselves, because they still live in the same house with them. Sadly, they have been deluded by Satan and have accepted his lie that it is okay to live in the non-intimate state of being roommates or worse, live as a present but covert enemy. If this is you, know that this is displeasing to God. You are emotionally torturing your wife. Some husbands convince themselves that they are still faithful to their wives even when they do not desire or pursue sexual intimacy with her. They cringe at the thought of sex with her but spend hours imbibing pornography. Brothers, if you are guilty of any of these selfish behaviors, they will keep you away from the *reprieve* response that is required for you to love your wife like Christ demands.

So, what does reprieve look like in marriage? It looks just like it did when God modeled it for Adam and Eve in Genesis 3:21. In an act of grace, God kills an animal, shedding its blood, and uses its skin to clothe Adam and Eve. In doing this, he covers their naked-ness, but more importantly, he shows them mercy. He reprieves them. That is, instead of punishing them fur-ther, he pardons them and brings them back into rela-tionship with Him. In a lesser, but similar way, Adam and Eve did the same for each other.

In spite of the devastating injury they inflicted upon each other in the Garden, Genesis 4:1 reveals that Adam and Eve evidently made the decision to stay with each other. When faced with the choice to reprieve each other or live in regret, they chose to love. They made up with each other. In fact, they made love. What would it take for you and your wife to get back to that kind of intimacy? I can imagine it involved Adam apologizing for his initial reaction and blame. I would think it also involved confession and repentance of his feelings of disdain. There is no doubt in my mind that getting back to intimacy was hard for him to do. And yet, it appears Adam did whatever it took to be reconciled to his wife. At the same time, I can imagine that Eve also apolo-gized for and owned her unfaithfulness in obeying the Serpent. Without a doubt, she had to work through her guilt and remorse to get back to intimacy.

The reprieve from God established Adam once again as God's representative, the husband, and the God-ordained head of his family. Adam's reprieve of Eve established her once again as "flesh of his flesh and bone of his bone," his soulmate and complementary image bearer. The giving and accepting of reprieve were essential to their healing and renewed relationship with each other and with God (Gen 4:1b). Without it, they would have suffered not only the loss of Eden but also the regret and permanent loss of each other. Their marriage was in crisis! Their relationship was on the rocks. Trust had been replaced with distrust. Love had been replaced with resentment. All their dreams and hopes were shattered. But romance God's way prevailed.

ROMANCE IS GOD'S IDEA, WITH REPRIEVING LOVE AS THE FOUNDATION.

Romance God's way is resilient, because it is built by granting reprieve, reaching out to bring your spouse back into oneness with you, over and over again— every time there is an infraction. Reprieve has equal parts mercy and love. It is like the love in Lamentations 3:22, 23: "The steadfast love of the Lord never ceases; His mercies never come to an end; they are new every morning; great is your faithfulness." This kind of mindset, the godly kind of mercy, love, and faithfulness, will enable us to pursue our wives. Romans 5:8 says that God pursues us, commending His love towards us while we were still sinners. Pursuing your wife looks like the self-sacrificing, "giving yourself up for her" type love we find in Ephesians 5:25. We are to demonstrate that kind of pursuing our wives: to romance them, to reprieve them, to bring them back when they fall short, and to win them even when they do not love us like we want or deserve. Likewise, we are to accept their reprieve when we sin—when we offend. Ultimately, we have the weighted responsibility. Husbands are commanded to be just like Christ who loved and retrieved us even when we were unlovable.

Romance God's way calls husbands to be like Christ in our marriages and homes.

Romance, God's way, is to love our wives by obeying God—to love by leading well in our homes and to love by hotly pursuing our wives only. Pray this prayer with me,

Lord, teach me to love you by obeying you. Let my growing obedience to you fuel my love for my wife. Create in me an increasing desire and ability to apply Scripture to my thinking. Help me show my love for her by leading her in the study of your Word. Teach me to pursue her in a way that delights her; increase my yearning after her and by doing that build a wall around my heart and blinders on my eyes. Help me Jesus, to romance my wife, like you pursue your Church. In Jesus name, I pray, amen.

We have established that marriage and the way we love our wives now are not the way they are supposed to be. We reviewed how it all went wrong. We suggested that our thinking is askew and needs to be righted. And we went so far as to demand that husbands need to hotly pursue their wives. In the following chapters, we will focus on how to turn "love your wives as Christ loves the Church," into observable behavior and consistent practice

CHAPTER 5

Transformed
Rather than Reformed

How can a husband change his behavior? How do we re-program our thinking? Some therapists would suggest psychotherapy and behavior modification strategies. In this book, we first turn to the Word of God as our guide, and then we will provide and apply strategies based on attachment theory. Theories can be useful only to the degree that they align with Scripture, and I believe John Bowlby's attachment theory does. For example, Bowlby, in his theory of child/parent attachment affirms what God said way back in the beginning, "It is not good for man to be alone." This statement expressed at the time man was created establishes what Bowlby explains in his theory: man has an innate need to be in relationship.

Staying in a relationship and being faithful in it, however, has become increasingly difficult for far too many husbands as we have already discussed in previous chapters. The problem, however, is not something that is happening to us; it is something that is happening inside of us. It is not an external issue, but an internal, spiritual one. Something is wrong with our hearts. Matthew 12:34 quotes Jesus as saying, "Out of the abundance of the heart the mouth speaks." In the same context, Jesus further cautions, ". . . the things that come out of the heart defile a man. For out of the heart proceed evil thoughts, murders, *adulteries, fornications,* thefts, false witness, blasphemies." Our thinking, Jesus says, reveals our nature. It displays who we are.

Scripture teaches that the heart speaks of the seat of our thinking. It is where our thoughts about God, self, and others take place. In the passage above, Jesus says our thinking is the origin of our behavior. Our good thinking leads to good behavior. Our bad thinking leads to bad behavior. Hence, how a husband thinks about his wife is likely to be how he behaves toward her. At the same time, a husbands' thinking and behavior towards his wife directly impacts a wife's thinking and behavior. In our research and experience, we have found this to be true.

For example, we surveyed two groups of wives: (W1) those who for the first time had experienced some trauma caused by their husband; and (W2) those whose husbands were ensnared in repeated and ongoing sin. We asked both sets of wives what one word would describe their marriages. The wives whose husbands were still struggling with adultery, alcoholism, or addiction to pornography were inclined to describe their marriages as "trying," "painful," "hopeless," and "on life support." In contrast, the wives, who had recently (in the last three months) seen a turnaround in their husband's behavior, were likely to use words such as "hopeful," "growing," "forgiving," and "loving."

We asked the husbands of these same women what word they would use to describe their marriages. Without us revealing to them what their wives had said, the husbands' responses provided insight into his thinking about himself, his wife, and his marriage. For instance, one husband who had just recently fallen back into destructive behavior, chose the word "painful," while his wife's word was "patience." Can you see how revealing the two words are? For the husband, it was painful because he had fallen yet another time. But the wife was committed to stay and endure the long hard road back for him.

Another husband, who walked a 10-year journey to overcome adulterous behavior, said, "Forgiveness." His wife said the same. This couple had done the hard work of forgiving and seeking forgiveness. They had both come to own and publicly testify to the damage both of them had done to their marriage. They had also made a commitment to daily seek to keep a zero balance of resentment. This means when offenses occurred, they were committed to work through them as immediately as they could muster up the courage and compassion to ask for and grant forgiveness. For this couple, "forgiveness" spoke of the environment they had cultivated in their relationship.

Our choice of words tells a story. They reveal not only what we are thinking but also predict how we are likely to behave. The words husbands chose, we found, were predictive of those who were likely to repeat their sin versus those who were truly repentant and less likely to repeat their sin. As Proverbs 23:7 says, "As a man thinks, so is he." What we say is what we think and is often predictive of what we are prone to do.

Here again, husbands, let me remind you, the heart is deceitful above all things and desperately wicked. Our heart is deceitful because we are sinners. We sin because it is in our un-redeemed nature to do so. At our core, we are prone to it. This is why Scripture never teaches that humans, husbands in this context, should work on being better. Even if we could be "better," our achievement would fall far short of God's standard. To please God as a husband takes a supernatural change of heart. Positive thinking and mindfulness are not the way to achieve loving our wives as Christ requires. We need a new internal working model—a transformed husband whose outward behavior originates from a renewed heart. Our very thought patterns need to change.

To be the husbands God demands requires the kind of transformation that changes us from the inside out. This type of change baffles the human mind. People initially doubt that it is real. It seems too good to be true. Wives are anxious to see it happen but often are doubtful at first when it does. It is the town drunk who becomes the self-sacrificing missionary, the slave ship captain who becomes the hymn writer and preacher, the previously unfaithful husband who turns from a wayward life to love and care for a bed-ridden wife, the absent, philandering, uncaring husband who experiences a heart change then turns to pursue and win back a wife who due to years of abuse has become apathetic, callous, and critical. This kind of change is only possible when we admit to our brokenness through the power of the

Holy Spirit and respond in faith to the saving power of Christ's life, death, and resurrection.

This is the kind of remarkable change Paul describes in Romans 12:1–2 where we read these words; "Brethren I implore you by the mercies of God that you present your bodies a living sacrifice, holy and acceptable unto God which is your reasonable service. Be not conformed to this world but be transformed by the renewing of your mind." At the end of this passage, Paul uses two Greek words which speak of change and behavior. The first word (*syschemetizo*) speaks of being conformed to a prescribed pattern or scheme (*schema*). This is outward behavior or change that does not reflect what is within. When Paul says in this verse, "Be not conformed to the world," he is emphatically telling Christians, including husbands, not to allow our thinking and behavior patterns to be like that of our sinful nature. He commands us not to act on the outside in a way that is different from the new nature Christ has given us. Simply put, do not be spiritually schizophrenic! Anytime we give in to our lust or carnal imagination, we are conforming to the world. We are acting just like unbelievers.

The other word (*metamorphoo*) speaks of being transformed—changed from the inside out. This change in a supernatural way defies and rises above what is humanly possible. This Scripture passage directs us to be transformed by the renewing of our minds. Our thinking and behaving need to be made new and different. Sinful man needs to be transformed, not reformed. Reformed sinners are yet in their sin. Transformed sinners are no longer slaves to sin. That is good news for every Christian husband.

Thank God, this good news, the gospel, eventually got a hold of my heart. This is the redemptive story as experienced in our marriage. You may find our story encouraging and convicting. This is the story of how God pursued me, pursued us, with patience and love.

KEN

I gave my heart to Christ one evening decades ago as a visiting missionary led me to Christ. I remember vividly the moment when my sinfulness and lostness became so clear to me that I cried out and asked Jesus to come into my heart and be my Savior. I was never quite the same again.

JUDY

For me, accepting Christ in my heart, meant that I had secured my place in heaven and all I needed to do was to follow the rules of Christianity. I attended church more often and went to Bible study, because in my mind, these were what the rules required.

You see, I thought I was a good person already. I brought this way of thinking and expectations into my marriage.

KEN

The early years of our marriage were about getting to know one another and having kids. Sadly, for me it became mostly about getting. I became an insatiable getter. And I was getting anything I put my mind toward. At the same time, resentment towards Judy was beginning to take root.

JUDY

Years passed, and we became, in my opinion, a successful family. I really admired Ken's work ethic and what he was able to achieve. I did my duty as a wife, mother, and teacher. We really looked the part, but beneath all the success, I was a broken woman driven by a critical spirit. Things had to be done my way. My way was perfect.

KEN

Our marriage deteriorated. Our nominal faith did not equip us to resist the Devil. I became the king of resentment. Angry and embittered, I saw Judy as the enemy. This fueled my sin which led to infidelity in our marriage. We agreed to separate.

JUDY

All that I had worked so hard to control was lost. I was no match for Satan. He had both of us right where he wanted us. His ultimate goal was to destroy, and he was gaining ground. I realized I was helpless. I needed greater power. The decisive moment for me came when my counselor said, "Judy, God has always been with you. You just haven't yielded to Him." For the first time I realized that I had accepted Christ as my savior but hadn't given him control in my life. I was doing it myself, living the rules of Christianity with selfish motives and self-righteous pride. My family had become my idol. Self-preservation, a critical spirit, and a high sense of responsibility were my strategies of control. But the love of God was missing from my heart.

KEN

God was not done with us or me yet. While separated from Judy, God continued convicting me and making me uncomfortable. I had no peace. I was unfulfilled, but my heart was hardened. Then something happened that began to change things. Judy's attitude towards me changed and caused me to wonder if there might be a chance for us. There was a strange but undeniable peace in the house when I visited. I was drawn to it— fully aware that I was not at peace in my own life.

JUDY

During the separation, for the first time I recognized my own spiritual condition. I was broken and needed Jesus to take control. I needed to trust Him. I finally surrendered control to the Lord. It took denying myself as it says in Matthew 16:24. It took letting everything go to find a life in Christ. It took Total Surrender. What did that mean for me? Here is the answer God gave me early one morning that changed my life: It's giving God the steering wheel in my life. His Word, Holy Spirit, and power are now the driving force (Philippians 4:13). It is an awareness of His hand in the choices I make today and every day. It's getting rid of all distractions so I can have time with the Lord. It is allowing Him to dwell richly in my mind and purify my thoughts. It's internalizing His word so I may put it into practice. It's trusting him for outcomes (Proverbs 3:5). It's loving in unimaginable ways, like being kind to Ken even though he'd hurt me so deeply. It's forgiving like Jesus Christ has forgiven me and in doing so being set free of bitterness and resentment. It's accepting love. It's giving Him my negative critical spirit and receiving in exchange the fruit of the Spirit: love, joy, peace, etc. It is not limiting God. It's the freedom to live fully each day in His presence, doing my duty out of love and service to Him. It is surrendering selfishness for selflessness, surrendering my control to His sovereignty for His honor and His glory in my Life.

KEN

Overnight, I found myself thinking of Judy in kinder, gentler ways. The more times I saw her, the more I saw the peace that she had, and the more I heard the voice of God speaking to my heart. His message was clear: I did not need a new marriage; I needed to let God make me a new man. That realization drove me to my knees, and I finally did what Mark 12:30 commands. I committed to Jesus all my heart, all my soul, all my mind, and all my strength. The next morning, I drove back to my God, my wife, my family, and my home. I immediately submitted to weekly accountability and discipleship with a veteran pastor, a Christian counselor, and three Christian brothers (who hold me accountable even now on a weekly basis). I gave up, years ago, my getting ways. I love my wife Judy, I love my kids, and I love my Lord. The resentment and rage are gone; I am freed from the mastery of sin; I am surrendered to God who is at work in me, to will and to do of His good purpose (Philippians 4:13).

The events mentioned above happened years ago. Today, God is using that experience to equip us to help others. We celebrate God's amazing love and grace toward us. We keep a zero account when it comes to resentment and negative criticism. We start every morning with prayer and Bible study. It is miraculous what He has done. We want you to know God can and is willing to do miraculous things in your life and marriage as well. Romans 8:28 is true. All things, every event, He will use for our good, His glory, and His purpose.

LOVE CAPTURES OUR HEARTS; AND MIRACULOUSLY SETS US FREE TO SERVE.

Our story could have had quite a different ending if I had my way. But in His mercy and by his grace, God did not let me have it. In my sinful state, I felt I needed a new woman, but in reality, I needed to become a new man. God did that for me. He pursued me. He convicted me of my sin. Then once I repented, He changed my heart and my desires. Pursuing your wife, husbands, involves letting Christ capture your heart. When he owns your heart, he transforms you. He gives you the desire to chase after your wife only. God pursued us. It is how God demonstrated His love for us. He pursued us with love even when we were running away from him (Romans 5:8).

He pursues us amidst our hurt, confusion, and sinfulness. He is our loving Shepherd who pursues us with goodness and mercy (Psalm 23). Like a lamb gone astray or a valuable lost coin, Jesus searches after us (Luke 15:3–10). He comes, knocking on our heart's door, wanting to be let in, as John writes in Revelation 3:20. Will you accept his pursuit of you—his reprieve, and turn back to him? Will you let him transform you from a 'not loving' husband into a loving one? Will you let him teach you how to love?

CHAPTER 6

Loving
Rather than Insecure

The next seven chapters provide instructions on how you may pursue and romance your wife God's way. This is not a list of activities that many of you already do, like giving flowers, buying chocolate, or ordering sexy lingerie—all of which are often superficial attempts to woo and seduce rather than authentic expressions of love and faithfulness. In the following pages, we focus on what it takes to be a Christian husband

and lover—one who is pleasing first to God and also to his wife.

So, can a 'not loving' husband become loving? As we began to show in the last chapter, the answer is yes. However, sometimes, it involves a journey back into childhood memories and hurts—one that most men are not likely to take. Brothers, fellow husbands, I implore you, understanding how past experiences taught you to love or not to love can help you serve God and love your wives better. What did this journey look like for Judy and me? What did it take for Judy, and more so for me, to surrender obedience to God and more lovingness towards one another? The following dialogue explains how the theory of attachment enabled Judy and me to come to understand our natural tendencies and understanding of love. The Lord used this understanding to help us love one another God's way.

JUDY

For me, the journey back started with me revisiting what I thought about marriage. Marriage for me, as I understood it, was more about doing my duty as a wife and mother. Of foremost importance to me was cleaning, cooking, and meeting the physical needs of my family. I was happy to finally have my own family—one that was not dysfunctional like the one I grew up in. At least that is what I thought until Ken had an affair. Devastated and shocked at the news of Ken's infidelity, I was numb and incredibly sad. The curse that I had seen in my parents' marriage had reared its ugly head in my own. Disgrace and shame were my initial feelings; however, they quickly became anger and resentment. Once again, I was betrayed and deserted by someone I loved.

KEN

For me, it took struggling to understand how I could profess faith in Christ while living very much like an unbeliever. Truth be told, I questioned my salvation. How can I be saved and so sinful? How do I make sense of walking away from my family and from God? I was at a loss—stuck in a quandary between my hypocritical behavior on one hand and my decades old claim of salvation on the other. How can I be saved and do what I had done?

Looking back now, I can see three phases God led me through to bring about my full surrender and restoration. The first phase involved recognizing the severity of my problem and realizing that only God can change my heart. The second involved owning and sharing my temptations, failures, and behaviors with trusted people who were walking with the Lord, who cared about me and were strong enough to deal with me. The third phase involved growing up spiritually, learning to endure suffering in a God-honoring and Spirit-led way.

JUDY

For me, it involved several decisions that would eventually change the nominal Christian life I had been living. First, I decided my marriage was no longer going to be the most important thing to me. Pleasing God became my highest priority. I wanted to know him intimately and for real. As I devoted more of my life to God, I stopped focusing so much on Ken and worrying whether he would stay this time or leave again. Instead, I surrendered him daily to God. Second, I enrolled in a discipleship program named Pure Life to work on my walk with the Lord. Finally, I decided that I did not want my old marriage back. Instead, I started praying and trusting God for His will for me. If he was calling me to live alone and serve Him, that was what I was going to do.

KEN

Remember, I said that the first phase involved owning the severity of my problem and recognizing that only God can change my heart? Here's what that looked like. As I mentioned above, the journey back to Christ led me back to my wife and family. Most significantly, however, it led me to examine my relationship with my birth mother. My earliest and prevailing memory of my mother was the day she gave me away as a 3-year-old to my aunt and uncle. For me, coming to own the severity of my sin meant coming to understand my sinful, anxious, and insecure attachment behavior. Persons with this type of attachment injury are likely to seek love in all the wrong places and in all the wrong ways. We are likely to easily detach from others. We are prone to either cling or be rigid in relationships. In marriage, this neediness and hardness are especially harmful and corrosive. It was in my marriage. I was the consummate insecure, controlling, and rigid lover. For the insecure anxious person like I was, marriage is a way to mercilessly demand what we want and need without any concern or desire to serve and care for the other person.

JUDY

I likewise had attachment, or should I say, detachment issues. Soon after my birth, I was adopted by my mother's cousin. However, my adopted mother and I never bonded. We never had mother-to-daughter conversations. I did not embrace her, nor did she embrace me. She never smiled. For a long time, neither did I. The only attention I got from her was based upon how well I did the daily housework assigned to me. By the time I was a teenager my understanding of self was distorted and self-effacing. I did not feel valuable, loved, or lovable. I was disaffected and unattached to others. It was me and me alone. In the language of attachment theory, I was avoidant and insecure. I did not expect others to love me, nor did I know how to love. I was so tainted that I rejected outright or was suspicious of any act of kindness or care offered by others. I did not think in terms of being loving or being loved. Instead, I saw myself as serving others to gain their approval, which explains why from age 14 through 18, when I lived with my birth mother, I did not attach as a family member. I saw myself as someone who was there to take care of others, while not being cared for myself.

KEN

The second phase as I mentioned, involved owning and sharing my temptations, failures, and behaviors with trusted people who were walking with the Lord, who cared about me and were strong enough to deal with me. Through the Holy Spirit's guidance, deep study of the Word, consistent and persistent prayer, and the help of trusted friends God revealed to me the root of my sinful behavior. Through the counsel of friends like Joe Enriquez, Gil Maycock, and Van Brown and studying books like Dallas Willard's *Spirit of the Disciplines* and J. I. Packer's *Knowing God,* I came to own that my understanding of God and salvation were deficient and inadequate for dealing with the depth and depravity of my sin. In fact, I wanted so much to understand what went wrong since my profession of faith, I decided to take a deep dive by enrolling in seminary. At seminary, I studied and became a qualified expert on God, attachment theory, and romantic attachment theory. God used these studies to change me—to bring me into a deeper walk with Him and into a fuller understanding of why I acted so desperately wicked in the past.

JUDY

Most of my life, I lived in the shadow of the little girl who was unloved and discarded—that is, until I was forced to make sense of how and why Ken left our marriage. Wrestling with the reality that I was once again deserted by someone who should have loved me brought me much despair and grief. However, in a painful and wonderful way, it was the turning point for me and my marriage. I, like Ken, came to realize I was suffering from attachment injury. In my case, it was the kind that kept me trying to earn the love of others, while at the same time believing that I would never really be loved. I too had been given away by my mother. My earliest memory of my birth mother was that of a beautiful woman visiting to bring me gifts at Christmas. Even though that was thoughtful, I did not feel loved by her, nor did I feel really loved by anyone. That is, until Ken left me, and I began to really seek after Christ. As I sought Him, I was led to do a deep study on love as revealed in the Bible. What I discovered changed my heart. For the first time, I began to experience what it means to receive and embrace love. God's love got ahold of me and freed me from the hurt that had ensnared me throughout my early life and during the course of our marriage. I began to love freely. I intentionally found ways to show my affection and love for Ken. I surprised my kids by doing the same for them. I did not realize it at the time, but God's love was beginning to work in and through me.

KEN

Fast forward to how my attachment injury played out in my marriage. I was not attached to Judy. I did not know how to be. After all, my primary attachment figure, my mother, the person from whom I would have learned to bond, to feel secure and safe—that very person had deserted me. Attachment disorder occurs when the primary caregiver is non-responsive and unavailable to the child. In fact, John Bowlby developed attachment theory by observing that the troubled young boys in his study all had one thing in common—a chronic lack of attention and care from their mothers. Since Bowlby, other researchers have found that the quality of attachment a person receives as a child creates an indelible imprint that affects romantic relationships later in life.

JUDY

So how did it all turn around for me—for us? What brought about our marriage miracle? For me, it all came together when I decided to open my Bible that had been sitting on my nightstand for years. I began to pray daily that God would change my heart and restore to me the joy of my salvation. I stopped praying for God's wrath to come down on Ken. Instead, I began praying for God's mercy and grace and that He would nudge Ken gently. I asked God to give me a new marriage—one in Him. Then after a year and a half, I began to understand and experience God purifying and refining me. First Peter 1:6–8 says,

> In this you greatly rejoice though now for a little while you may have to suffer grief in all kinds of trials. These have come so that your faith- of greater worth than gold which perishes even though refined by fire may be proved genuine and may result in praise, glory and honor when Jesus Christ is revealed. Though you have not seen Him, you love Him, and even though you do not see Him now, you believe in Him and are filled with an inexpressible joy.

God was now first in my life, no matter the circumstances. For me, this became an irreversible commitment. To my surprise, at a time when it pleased the Lord, He brought Ken back. He resurrected a dead marriage, turned ashes into beauty, and now together we walk in newness of life in Christ to the honor and praise of Him. Because of an intimate relationship with Christ and total reliance on Him, God has given me the power to love Ken in the way He designed me to.

KEN

The third phase for me involved growing up spiritually, learning to endure suffering in a God-honoring and Spirit-led way. God by His Grace brought me to a moment when I came to understand that my attachment disorder is my cross to bear. It is the kind of sin scar that, if left untreated, could grow into a cancer, eventually destroying a person. Or it could, once a person turns to God, bring about godly discipline and spiritual maturity. To see it as such, and by God's grace I did, I came to see my failure to attach as sin and because of sin, not merely my sin or my mother's sin, but Adam's sin as well. God opened my eyes. I was finally able to make sense of my sinful ways. I am a sinner, prone to act out and express Adam's nature in specific ways that reflect the attachment disorder passed onto me by my mother who had her own set of attachment issues.

Long before attachment theory was developed, the Genesis account records how attachment disorder entered humanity. Healthy, secure attachment existed between Adam and Eve and between God and man in the beginning in the Garden. Then man sinned, and attachment was distorted between God and Adam and Eve. For me, seeing my attachment issues through the biblical narrative helped me understand afresh why Christ died. He died to give me a new nature, because the one I got from Adam was killing me (Romans 5:12). Christ died to free me from sin and to give me a relationship with Him that overcomes my attachment disorder. He died to re-connect me to God. Romans 5:10 explains it this way: "For if when we were enemies, we were reconciled (re-connected) to God through the death of His son, much more having been reconciled (re-connected), we shall be saved by His life." Christ died that my attachment needs would be completely satisfied in Him. Once that truth took hold of me and got ahold of Judy, our thinking and behavior began to change.

We are no longer needy, weak, and yearning for love. We know without a doubt we are attached to Him. He is our safe haven, our peace. He is always available and accessible to us (Matthew 28:20).

- Our desires and appetite are most often pleasing and glorifying to him. We desire to read His Word daily (1 Peter 2:2).
- Our reactions are more likely to be kind and thoughtful. I am sensitive to Judy's needs, and she is sensitive to mine (Philippians 2:3).
- We confess our sins more immediately. We are quick to pray (James 5:16).
- We ask for forgiveness more readily (1 John 1:9).
- I see my past behavior as evil and wicked. She agrees and loves me just the same (Ephesians 5:8).
- Love is no longer what I seek only to get, but more so what I seek to give. Love is me investing in Judy for her benefit, and she is doing the same for me (1 Corinthians 13:4–8).

Christianity is not merely what we say or claim now; it is our lifestyle. Our behavior is Christ-centered: we guard our hearts and control our tongues. Our thinking is Christ-centered: we set our minds on things above, first thing every morning. Our worldview is Christ-centered: we reject the world's version of love and romance and are learning that love is patient and kind. Our ambition is Christ-centered: we live for Christ, not our culture, politics, or our family name. Our identity is Christ-centered: we endure suffering to become holy and seek to walk worthy of his calling, to represent Christ, to be His ambassadors. Like Paul, I, Ken, create patterns to subject my body to keep my desires holy—to prevent my eyes and heart from ever wandering again.

The following are five patterns we have set for our marriage:

1. Start every day by putting Jesus before each other. Read His word and talk to Him first.
2. In daily events, trust God immediately.
3. Be the safest, most reliable person on earth for your spouse.
4. Keep a zero account of resentment and a full tank of forgiveness.
5. Live like Christ and love the sinner—especially the one right next to you.

ROMANCE IN ADULTHOOD IS LIKELY TO MIMIC LOVE LEARNED IN CHILDHOOD.

This is the information we share in our *ReEngage* marriage ministry. You may have noticed a key theme in our testimony: God pursued two adopted kids with severe attachment issues. We thank God that by His grace, both Judy and I came to understand that we were fraught with attachment issues. And we are not alone. About 50 percent of the U.S. population struggles with some form of attachment insecurity. In your marriage, there is a possibility that you or your spouse are either anxious-insecure or avoidant-insecure.

Anxious-Insecure vs. Avoidance-Insecure

The anxious-insecure person holds on tightly to their spouse for fear of losing them. The avoidant person refuses to depend on their spouse for the same reason—for fear of losing them. In both instances, the concern is that our spouse may not stay. In the first instance, our experience as a child taught us that we need to work hard to make the person love us. This results in a compelling need to cling. In the second, our experience has imprinted upon us that people are not likely to care about us or love us anyway, so why get attached? This results in a self-defacing conviction that we are unlovable and do not deserve to be loved.

Sadly, many people, maybe even you, husband, live this skewed understanding of self and others. It is possible that until now, you have not connected how you behave towards your wife to how you were loved or not loved as a child. I know I did not. I never thought childhood experiences, even the painful ones, could have residual impact on my behavior. If something does not kill you, it makes you stronger, right? Not always. Some early experiences can injure you. When hurts are left unidentified and unattended, you maneuver through life with an emotional limp, but you think it is your unique way of walking. It is not; it is unresolved pain that is fueling your tendency to not love.

The good news is that "love is patient; love is kind; love does not envy; it does not boast; it is not proud; it does not dishonor others; it is not self-seeking; it is not easily angered; it keeps no record of wrongs; love does not delight in evil but rejoices in the truth. It always protects, always trusts, always hopes, always perseveres." This is good news for those of us who are insecure. Paul delivered this news to a group of Christians who had witnessed love gone wrong in the Corinthian church. Paul refers to the good news in 1 Corinthians 13:4–8 as "a more excellent way" to live in relationship with others (1 Corinthians 12:31). We can be loving rather than insecure in our love.

CHAPTER 7

Patient
Rather than Self-Gratifying

To love is to be patient by calmly waiting, enduring, and suffering. To love patiently is to endure months of uncertainty—like the ones right after Judy and I came back together. To love patiently is Judy staying in the marriage even when each time she looked at me, she was reminded of how badly I hurt her. To love patiently is me not running away again even when I feared that I had hurt her so badly that I questioned whether she would ever be able to forgive me. For both of us, "love is patient" means persevering, staying the course. It means enduring the pain of building a different kind of marriage—one built on obeying the Word of God. The Greek word Paul uses for "patient" in 1 Corinthians 13:4 is *markrothymeo,* which means "longsuffering" or "long-tempered."[5] It is the act of remaining tranquil while waiting. It is having a mind at peace even when provoked. John MacArthur explains:

> The word is common in the New Testament and is used almost exclusively of being patient with people, rather than with circumstances or events. Love's patience is the ability to be inconvenienced or taken advantage of by a person over and over again and yet not be upset or angry.[6]

The behavior MacArthur describes is noticeably uncommon. Patience is not commonly modelled today. It is not commonly on display in society, nor is it on display regularly in our relationships. *Psychology Today* explains, "Today more than ever, patience is a forgotten virtue. Our individualistic and materialistic society values ambition and action (or, at least, activity) above all else, whereas patience involves a withdrawal and withholding of the self."[7] This article defines patience as the promotion of others above self, the withholding of putting yourself before or above the other person.

Christianity Today provides this insight about why patience is so difficult for us in relationships: "All human beings are sinners and therefore selfish and annoying. But a psychological explanation also helps to explain why patience is so challenging. It concerns what philosophers call the 'egocentric predicament,' which is the natural human condition of being immediately aware only of one's own thoughts and feelings."[8] A selfish me-focus is at the root of why we are naturally disposed to being impatient. The article goes on to show the alternative impact patience has upon relationships: "Patience amounts not to mere restraint or toleration, but to an active, complicit engagement in [others'] struggle and welfare. In that much, patience is a form of compassion, which, rather than disregarding and alienating people, turns them into friends and allies."[9] Patience, although hard to come by, is noticeably powerful in bringing about positive change in our relationships.

In summary, these two articles, John MacArthur's observation and the Greek definition of "patient," point to this conclusion: "love is patient" leads to delaying, if not denying one's own comfort, convenience, or needs, in order to help another person get what they need.

This sounds like self-sacrificing love. This sounds like what Christ did for us. Being patient provides husbands with a grand opportunity to love their wives like Christ loves his church. Make this your ambition. Make loving your wife patiently your goal. Do this, and you will reap the unique rewards that patience brings. Patience positively impacts the effectiveness of your courting, foreplay, and lovemaking. As you read further in this chapter, keep this in mind, husbands, who long to obey God more and love their wives better must:

Patiently study.
Patiently listen.
Patiently touch.
Patiently discuss.
Patiently, thoroughly enjoy.

Patiently Study

Wives often express how they wish their husbands would talk to them more or talk to them more openly. When we ask husbands to explain why they do not talk more, husbands generally do not know what to talk about. They do not know their wives well enough to talk about what is interesting, troubling, or meaningful to her. Is this you? Do you know what to talk to your wife about that impacts your love life positively? Are your conversations likely to increase intimacy in your marriage? Here are some questions that can help you determine the quality of your conversations with your wife:

- What is most pressing and of immediate concern to your wife right now?
- How does she need you to show your love to her today?
- What topic does she wish she could talk to you about but is afraid that you will blow up, shut her down, or try to fix it?
- What do you do during love-making that is unpleasant or a turn off for her?
- Would she describe you as an impatient or patient lover?

Chances are you may be able to answer the first question, because she is always talking about it. The other questions, however, require that you study her. These deeper and more hidden needs require patient and targeted observation. The problem is most husbands do not study their wives. We are not loving her in that way. Maybe the last time we invested in knowing our wives was early on in our marriage. During those early moments when we were yet uncertain about whether we truly liked each other or not or still unsure of what we would be like as a couple, we set aside time to get to know her. We were motivated to try to discover what she liked, how she was feeling, and what mattered to her.

Now we have her and are confident of her love. Now we have relaxed and lost that kind of interest. That does not have to be the case. We can change. Here are a few questions that can help us engage more with our wives:

- How does your wife want to be pursued by you?
- What tells her that you are into her?
- What words signal to her that she is beautiful and desirable to you?
- What are your answers?
- How confident are you that your answers are what she would say?

Rather than just asking her, find out the answers to these questions by studying her, watching her, listening to her, and asking God to reveal the answer. Watch her body language and non-verbal cues more. You probably already recognize the non-verbal cues when you have offended her or failed to do what you promised or what she asked you to do. Now, instead start studying the cues for when she is hurting and needs you to hurt with her. Become good at knowing how to comfort her when your teenagers yell at full volume how much they hate her. Or better yet, learn from those instances when you fail to be nice or caring, and she points out your error by saying nothing—nothing at all. Study her. Get to know her again. Take the next seven days, and put this process of studying your wife on your daily to-do list. Get to know what thoughts rush at her first thing in the morning. Study her after love-making—Can you tell if she is satisfied or not? If she is, make a mental note of what made it go so well.

Patiently Listen

In our couple sessions, many wives say their husbands do not listen. Along with patiently studying your wife, you should love her by patiently listening. Become known as her listening partner. Unabashedly show that you are actively listening. Let her know with your comments and questions that you hear her and are interested in what she is saying. Ask her to rephrase or explain what she is saying when you do not understand. Go further and set aside regular and daily times when you will put aside your smart devices and turn off the television to listen to her.

Listening by the way, can be a very important aspect of your love-making ritual, especially if she was not satisfied. Remember how we said patience reveals things about the person being patient, and that it also reveals things to the person with whom you are being patient? Patiently communicating after lovemaking did not end with mutual satisfaction reveals that you are safe—that the relationship is secure. For your wife, your patience informs her that she can trust you; she can be transparent with you. In this way, post-love-making becomes a precious time of transparency—a time to establish yourself as a haven for your wife. She will find it easier to talk to you about when sex did not work when you are lovingly patient. She is more likely to discuss options for making it better next time when you are calm and reassuring. Husbands, patiently listening to your wife allows her to tell you exactly how she needs you to love her and reveals how she wants you to *make love to her.*

Patiently Touch

I intentionally delayed addressing the lovemaking 'touch aspect' of studying your wife after the listening section because patiently loving your wife reorganizes the priority most husbands employ when seeking to romance their wives. In most marriages, husbands have trained their wives that when he starts touching, in the words of the wives, "He wants something." To apply "love is patient" to your marriage, husbands, you will need to re-teach your wife and re-train yourself. You will need to replace the idea of touching her as a means to get what you want and practice touching her to give her what she needs.

Wives first want non-sexual touching from their husbands. Most times, she just wants you to pull her gently to your chest and hold her. Let her feel your heart beating next to hers. Let her exhale in your warm embrace. Just be still with her. So go ahead and touch her, hold her hand, rub her back, and tell her (and mean it) that you do not want sex. You just want to comfort her and love her by touching her in a non-sexual way. When it is time for sexual intimacy, remember once again to listen to her. Does she like what you are doing? Listen to her breathing, suspend your own satisfaction as you patiently wait for her. Be her patient lover.

Patiently Discuss

More than any other issue, it seems most marriages are in trouble because of communication issues. One reason for that is spouses are unable or unwilling to engage in constructive and respectful discussions. Husbands can take the lead by patiently discussing these five most prominent topics couples face: finances, sex, child discipline, in-laws, and blended family issues.

An effective way for a husband to patiently discuss difficult and emotional topics with his wife is by understanding the WENI acronym and process. This diagnostic tool developed by Scott Stanley, Daniel

Trathen, Savanna McCain, and Milt Bryan can help a husband identify what he needs to stop doing to have more lovingly patient discussions with his wife. These authors use the WENI acronym to teach four 'not loving' behaviors husbands must monitor, manage, and minimize in order to be more lovingly patient in discussions.[10] A husband must avoid:

- **W**ithdrawal: This is an unwillingness to get into or stick with important discussions. This can be as obvious as leaving the room in the middle of a conversation or as subtle as shutting down emotionally.

- **E**scalation: This occurs when you respond negatively toward your spouse and the conversation continues to get more and more hostile. You may immediately think of escalation as a husband or wife (or both) yelling and screaming at each other, and it can often happen that way. But you can also escalate in more subtle ways—sarcasm, name-calling, threats, and other forms of attack. You can do a lot of damage to your marriage in a short period of time if you are an escalator.

- **N**egative interpretation: This happens when you assign a motive to your spouse that is more negative than is really the case. Negative interpretation can also look like you asking a question and your spouse interpreting it as a negative statement. Oftentimes, people will negatively interpret in areas where there is some insecurity or if veiled comments were common in their family growing up.

- Invalidation: This occurs when you directly or indirectly dismiss, minimize, or put down the thoughts, feelings, or character of your spouse. It can look like picking apart your spouse's opinions or feelings instead of being sensitive and trying to understand their point of view.

Embracing this process is a really good way to let 'love is patient' revamp your communication style.

Patiently, Thoroughly, Enjoy

Love is patient is when you, as her husband, focus on serving your wife and choose to delay or deny your desires. Not loving patiently, on the other hand, is focusing on getting what you want, prioritizing you, and feeling rather annoyed, even angry, that your wife is not giving you what you need. Willard Harley Jr., in his book *His Needs, Her Needs,* makes this observation:

Couple after couple explained to me that they married each other because they found each other irresistible—they were in love. By the time they came to my office they had lost that feeling for each other. In fact, many were finding each other downright repulsive. When I asked them, "What would it take for you to be happily married again?" most couldn't imagine that ever happening. But when I persisted and couples were able to reflect on my question, the answer I heard repeated over and over was, "for us to be in love again."[11]

Fellow husbands, is that what you want? Do you want to know that your wife is in love with you again? Do you want to be in love with her again? Then, start here: start with knowing that love is active. Every time we see love in Scripture or in life, we can observe it because it is never only a feeling. Love is demonstrated and observable. We know when someone loves us, and they know when we love them. How do we know? By their actions—love is displayed in what we do and how we do it.

In summary, to fully understand the 'love is patient' type of love, we must return to what being patient reveals about the person showing patience and what it conveys to the person needing patience. Patience in a person, as we read in the *Christianity Today* article, reveals that they are compassionate and longsuffering. Longsuffering, as the word suggests, involves suffering over a period of time. Patience is never quick and easy. We observe a person being patient in a situation where it would be normal to not have patience amid trying circumstances when it is observably painful to be calm. Scripture does not say love enjoys; it says love endures (1 Corinth 13:7). Incorporating how love 'does patient' into how you react to your wife is where you have an untapped opportunity to romance her.

Patience in a person reveals important things to the person with whom you are being patient. Patience towards a person shows them that you care. Patience towards a person shows that they can depend upon you. Patience towards your wife indicates to her that she can count on you being there not only when you need her, but reassuringly, when she needs you. Husbands, patiently loving is an aspect of romance that too many of us are failing to employ.

After all, God's design is for sex in marriage to be God-honoring and thoroughly enjoyable (Hebrews 7:26). Enjoy making love to your wife because this is God's perfect will for you. He has given her to you both for your pleasure and hers. Study her patiently to learn how to please her thoroughly by actively listening to her. Delay your own pleasure by touching her in a way that serves and pleases her. Bask in the afterglow by initiating and engaging in discussions about what worked or did not work during sexual intercourse. Pursue your wife patiently and thoroughly enjoy her.

CHAPTER 8

Love is Kind
Rather than Unkind

K indness is proactive. We initiate kindness. It is our choice, our idea. It cannot be demanded or coerced; it is freely and thoughtfully given. The Greek word for kindness, in 'love is kind' is *chrēsteuomai*, which is an action word meaning love is considerate and does kindness towards another. MacArthur in this regard writes,

> The Christian husband who acts like a Christian is kind to his wife and children. Christian

brothers and sisters are kind to each other and to their parents. They have more than kind feelings toward each other; they do kind, helpful things for each other—to the point of loving self-sacrifice, when necessary.[12]

Kindness as the Greek defines it and as MacArthur describes it is not random. It is intentional. Kindness is a choice. We choose to surprise someone with a kind gesture. We decide to respond in a kind way. We choose to consider another's feelings. Kindness happens first within.

KINDNESS IS AN INTERNAL HEALTHINESS THAT MANIFESTS IN EXTERNAL HELPFULNESS.

It flows from the condition of our hearts—our state of mind. When we are in a 'kindness state-of-mind,' we are sensitive to the needs of others. We are proactive, even creative, in serving them.

Ever noticed a couple in love and how they behave? They are kind to each other. They are proactive towards each other. He is opening doors to let her go in first. She is sitting, rubbing his back. He is looking at her, attentively as she talks. In contrast, ever noticed the behavior of a couple in trouble? Their body language communicates unkindness towards each other. They are purposefully not touching, not sharing their space, and not connecting to each other. They are not thinking of the next kind thing they can do for each other.

Kindness is a heart condition that shows up in our behavior. So why did Paul need to command the Christians in the early church to "be kind to one another?" (Ephesians 4:32). Why did he have to say it? Could it be that we are not naturally kind? Or could it be that kindness requires us to be intentional? Could it be that he is affirming the presence of the Holy Spirit and the fruit of kindness He produces in us? Yes.

By Adam's nature, we are prone to be unthoughtful or inconsiderate towards others. In our flesh, we are inclined to be selfish and self-centered. In Christ, however, we are commanded and empowered to be kind (Galatians 5:22). The fact is, we choose if we obey our flesh and respond to our wives in unkind ways. Or we choose to obey the Holy Spirit and respond with kindness. Paul David Tripp, in his book *Instruments in The Hand of The Redeemer*, makes this statement: "Our lives are shaped by indulging the sinful nature or by self-sacrificing love."[13] We choose to live one way or the other. In the same way, our choices determine the shape of our marriages. This is especially true when we are regularly embroiled in emotional and heated debates with our wives. During these times, we often say things that cut deeply and indelibly. Before we realize it, over time, our marriage has devolved into a recurring pattern of unkind behavior.

In this context, Tripp challenges Christians with the following questions: "In the face of powerful emotions and desires, what will we do? As sons and daughters of the King, will we live in self-imposed bondage to our emotions? Will we submit to the mastery of our sinful desires? Or will we grab hold of the promises of the gospel and turn in a completely different direction?"[14] These can be convicting questions according to how we are walking with God and each other.

Sadly, Judy and I have had notable unkind and kind moments when we have been convicted and reminded that our hearts are now under new management. One such moment was a recent trip to our local Walmart. Here's what happened: Judy and I were in the checkout line when the gentleman ahead of us was having problems getting his credit card to work. This was admittedly an 'impatience inducing moment' for both of us.

Finally, it was our turn. As the cashier finished, I put in my card and inadvertently hit the cancel key instead of the enter key. Immediately Judy pushed me aside with her elbow saying, "Move out the way. Let me do this." I was livid. She paid the bill and walked off with me silently fuming and stalking behind her.

When she did not remember where we parked, I said nothing and let her walk the wrong way.

My 'not loving self' had taken over. I went to where the car was without letting her know. She ended up about two lanes across a median, lost. Finally, she noticed me standing in the distance next to our car. I watched her struggle to get the full grocery cart up and over the embankment. When she arrived, she said, in one long breath, "You saw me going the wrong way, and you saw me struggling with the cart—I was wrong for how I behaved at the cashier earlier." Her apology diffused my anger. I confessed I was wrong also and could have reacted differently. We rehashed the event and confessed and forgave each other.

Our reaction to this situation was very different than it has been in the past. Before, this would have been another negative experience added to the putrid pile of venomous resentment. Instead, we disarmed the situation. Kindness is now, particularly after we have been unkind, our default behavior. We have learned all too well that when we are angry and resentful, it is hard to be kind. When we are self-centered instead of God-centered, we can be cold-heartedly unkind. Husbands, be warned—unkindness reveals selfish 'not-loving' behaviors which are likely to have an indelible and destructive impact upon your marriage.

In fact, unkindness in marriage can foreshadow impending doom. According to John Gottman, unkind negative behavior is a predictor of marriages prone to failure.[15] Marriages that fail, according to Gottman, violate an observable 5-to-1 magic ratio. This "magic ratio," according to Gottman, is based on research that revealed a healthy marriage will have one negative interaction compared to five (or more) positive interactions. This suggests that healthy marriages have loving spouses, rather than not-loving spouses, who consequently are five times more likely to be kind in word and behavior. When we are loving our spouse, we are in a 'kindness-state-of-mind,' which makes us sensitive to their needs.

This is the type of 'need-sensitive' kindness Willard Harley Jr. focuses on in his book, *His Needs, Her Needs*. He makes this observation: "Even though sexual fulfillment and recreational companionship are statistically less important to women than they are to men, women in love tend to fulfill [her husband's] needs almost effortlessly. Similarly, the [wife's] needs of affection and intimate conversation are met almost effortlessly by a man in love. It's as if their instincts to meet these needs kick in as soon as they are in love."[16]

When we are in love, according to Harley, we proactively fulfill each other's needs. Wow! What a thought! Kindness is a normal and conspicuous part of loving. This is what the Bible teaches. God loves us. Therefore, He was and is kind to us; He gave us His

Son (John 3:16). He demonstrated His love toward us (Romans 5:8).

Loving kindness is always demonstrated and visible. We can observe when someone loves us, and they can see when we love them. How so? By their actions and ours—love is displayed in how considerate we are, how giving we are, and how kind we are. Are you kind to your wife? When was your most recent kindness toward her? What did you do? Do you have a kind relationship?

Fellow husband let's make our marriage filled with kindness. Let's strive to make kindness the rule rather than the exception. Make it such that when an infraction occurs, as in our Walmart story, we quickly show kindness by forgiving each other. Scripture commands us to "be kind to one another, tender hearted, forgiving one another, as God in Christ forgave you" (Ephesians 4:32). This verse is a command: being kind is not optional for the husband who is obedient to God. This verse is also instructive; it gives us three steps to follow in order to practice kindness toward our wives:

Step 1: Soften Your Heart

Ephesians 4:32 commands us to be tenderhearted. The Greek word used is, *eusplagchnos,* which means to be compassionate, to share in another person's hurt feelings. MacArthur describes tenderheartedness as "a feeling deep in the bowels, or stomach, a gnawing psychosomatic pain due to empathy for someone's need."[17] We are to be compassionate, to feel the other person's hurt. That is how God loves—Scripture says of Jesus, "He is touched with the feelings of our infirmities" (Hebrews 4:15). Christ's heart is soft towards us. He is lovingly affectionate toward us. Men, sadly, often the same cannot be said for many of us. Are you affectionate? No, I am not talking about when you want sex. Would your wife say that you are soft-hearted toward her?

Wives in our marriage sessions regularly say how they wished their husbands would show more affection. They do not want their husbands to be less masculine or more feminine. They are wanting and needing from us a side of love that most men are not used to showing. They are yearning for what Gary Smalley and John Trent in their book, *The Two Sides of Love*, call the soft side of love. Fellow husbands, when the Bible tells us, "Love is kind," it is asking us to show the soft side of love in our marriage. Smalley and Trent define soft-sided love:

> Softside love is a tenderness that grows to be the same color as unconditional love. When held in balance, it manifests characteristics like

compassion, sensitivity, patience, and understanding. It's the sympathy of a father who sits with his arm around his daughter as she cries over a lost boyfriend, without even a hint of a lecture or an "I told you so." It's the encouragement of a mother whose cheerful "You can do it!" email arrives just before her son's medical school entrance exams. And it's the kindness of a man who still calls his best friend's parents each year on the day their son died in Iraq—just to let them know he remembers and that their son will never be forgotten by his friend. Softside love takes time to understand another's feelings and listens instead of lecturing. It shows itself in the willingness to reach out and warmly touch and hug someone.[18]

There are instances where husbands and fathers are likely to demonstrate the soft side of love. We can be kind, compassionate, and affectionate. However, we must choose to do so regularly and consistently.

Step 2: Make it Safe

In the first part of Colossians 3:19, we are told how we are to love our wives. We are to love our wives in a continuous unfailing way. MacArthur, commenting on this verse, writes:

The present tense of the imperative agapate (love) indicates continuous action. The verb itself seems best understood in the New Testament to express a willing love, not the love of passion or emotion but the love of choice—a covenant kind of love. It could be translated "keep on loving."[19]

Once we are married, we always are to be loving to our wives. Today, tomorrow, and every day is supposed to be a day of loving behavior toward her. Doing so showcases the work that God has done and is doing in our hearts as Christian men. "A Christian home," Dr. Tony Evans writes, "is not just a place where some Christians reside; it's where the authority of Jesus Christ rules the participants of a family."[20]

Being loving toward our wives is evidence that we are under His rule. We are obeying His Word and placing ourselves under His authority. Doing so communicates to our wives that it is safe to submit to us (Colossians 3:18,19). Consistent, loving, kind behavior over time lets her know she can trust you. Colossians 3:19 paints the picture of ever increasing, always happening, consistently loving and serving our wives. "A kingdom man then," Dr. Evans suggests, "is not a dictator, ruling his home with a heavy hand and expecting his family to wait on him. Instead, he is a benevolent leader under the authority of God, acting with love and seeking the well-being of his wife and children."[21] The Christian man demonstrates 'love is kind' by taking care of his wife and family.

Step 3: Forgive Quickly

The first part of the verse tells us how to love. The second part of the verse, however, warns against that which inhibits us from loving. What is so powerful, so disruptive, that it can derail loving behavior? Paul indicates in this verse that bitterness is a destructive force when allowed to grow in a marriage. The Greek word Paul uses is *pikrainō*. It is in the imperative as if Paul is shouting, "Stop it! Turn away! Don't do it! Do not become embittered; do not allow resentment to fester. If you do, you are no longer loving." To heed this verse, we need to practice forgiving quickly. Forgiving is an act of kindness. We are compassionate and considerate when we forgive. We are being kind when we take steps to prevent resentment from taking root.

Theologian and veteran pastor Warren Wiersbe adds this commentary about Colossians 3:

> Paul added a special word of warning for the husbands: "And be not bitter against them" (Col. 3:19). Husbands must be careful not to harbor ill will toward their wives because of something

they did or did not do. A "root of bitterness" in a home can poison the marriage relationship and give Satan a foothold (Eph. 4:31; Heb 12:15).

A happy marriage does not come automatically; it is something that must be worked on all the time. As we walk with Christ in submission to Him, we have no problem submitting to one another and seeking to serve one another. But where there is selfishness, there will be conflict and division. If there is bitterness in the heart, there will eventually be trouble in the home. Where do we get the power to love and to submit? From the Lord . . . . If we live to please Christ first, others second, and ourselves last, we will build strong marriages and spiritual homes.[22]

Wiersbe advises husbands to not let bitterness harbor. The best way to prevent this is by being submissive, having a willingness to forgive quickly. I confess, and you already know this about me from the Walmart story, forgiving quickly is an area in which I need to grow. I wrestle, regrettably so, to not hold resentment.

This is where our wives can help. When needed, Judy reminds me that we agreed to keep a zero balance when it comes to resentment. We agreed that when unkindness shows up, one of us, usually the one who is being less selfish and more obedient to God, will take the first step to stop resentment. Judy did this with me at Walmart. She helped me. She took the first step that helped us zero-out resentment. Only then were we willing and able to forgive quickly and fully. Love is being kind; it is forgiving and submitting to each other.

CHAPTER 9

Love Promotes Truth Rather than Self

W hat was Adam's fateful failure in the Garden? Was it because he ate the fruit? Was it because the Serpent deceived him? No, "the Serpent deceived Eve by his cunning" (2 Corinthians 11:3). First Timothy explains, "Adam was not the one deceived; it was the woman who was deceived and became a sinner" (1 Timothy 2:14). Adam was not tricked by the Devil. Eve was. He ate the fruit Eve offered him, but that was not his major downfall. THE grave sin Adam committed, the sin that toppled him, and sadly, is still toppling men today, is failure to lead his wife according to God's Word. Adam knew the Truth. He knew God's command to him. God had made it clear to him. He schooled Adam at the very beginning of their relationship as to what was pleasing and displeasing to him. He created Adam first to be the standard bearer for Eve and for all humanity. Thus, sin did not spread to the human race when Eve ate the fruit. But Adams' complicit response to Eve's transgression infected every human for all history.

When Eve took that first bite, time stood still. When she turned and offered the forbidden fruit to Adam, all creation held its breath, waiting to see what her husband would do. What would God's sub-regent, the first created being, God's hand-picked representative—what would he do? This was a leadership challenge—an opportunity for Adam to shine. This was a family crisis—a time to lead his family in repentance, to re-group and reassert God's rightful authority in the home. What did Adam as the head of household have the power and responsibility to do? What could he have done differently? He could have said, "No Eve you have done wrong. We do not love God by disobeying. We love Him by obeying." He could have reminded her of God's Word. He could have lovingly guided his wife back to the Truth. He could have loved her by loving God and obeying God's command. Instead, "Sin came into the world through one man, [Adam] and death through sin, and so death spread to all men" (Romans 5:12).

Adam failed to step up and be the obedient, promise-keeping, helpful partner to Eve. She and all humans needed Adam's love for God at that moment. But he failed to love God and Eve by failing to live and obey God's truth. He surrendered his God-given role as leader and protector of Eve who had obviously gone astray. Tony Evans puts it this way:

> Satan caused their roles to be reversed, approaching Eve with his deception while Adam stood silently by and watched. Though he was supposed to take an active role in watching over the garden and keeping God's command (Gen. 2:15-17), Adam became passive, allowed the devil to tempt Eve, and then knowingly followed her into sin. Importantly, though Eve was deceived, Scripture lays responsibility for humankind's fall into sin at the feet of Adam.[23]

Adam, in a 'not loving' way, failed to live what 1 Corinthians 13:6 teaches: love "rejoices in the truth." Loving requires us to embrace, encourage, and correct with God's Word when our spouse is in trouble. Evans explains that "Love does not affirm someone in their sin or their false beliefs because love finds no joy in unrighteousness but rejoices in the truth."[24] By eating the fruit with Eve, Adam affirms her sin instead of confronting it. This was 'not loving.' Husbands, this is a game changer.

We are to love God much more than we love our wife. We are to love Him in such a way that our behavior helps her grow in her faith. Ephesians 5 alludes to us presenting our wives in the same way Christ presents and sanctifies his Church. We are to help our wives with sanctification. Evans explains,

> A kingdom husband is to be his wife's sanctifier—taking her (and all her history) from where she is and helping her to where she ought to be, just as Christ sanctifies the church. A kingdom husband out-serves his wife. Even as a husband loves himself, he is to love his wife—giving her his strength and encouragement. The goal is to facilitate transformation through the influence of love.[25]

Fellow husbands, what is it like to be married to you? Is it a sanctifying experience? Are you spending time in God's Word with your wife? Are you loving her in such a way that she is maturing as a Christian? How are you helping your wife grow in her love for Christ? Evans adds,

> Far too many men think headship means playing dictator and telling everyone what to do. But biblical headship means being a responsible governing authority. The husband is responsible for leading his family in the advancement of God's kingdom in the context of love. Biblical love compassionately, righteously, and sacrificially pursues the well-being of another. The man, then has got to move first. When a woman sees her man initiating, owning responsibility, treating her as special, and sacrificing for her well-being, she is apt to respond to him with heartfelt respect and submission.[26]

So how can we 'rejoice in the truth" in our marriage? We can start by reviewing our expectations regarding marriage to ensure that they align with God's truth.

Each spouse comes into marriage with things they expect to get and give. This was certainly the case for Adam and Eve. Let's go back to the Garden. When Adam said within Eve's hearing, you are "bone of my bones, and flesh of my flesh," what may she have been expecting from him? Do you think she expected that he would step in to help when she needed it? Do you think she expected that he would share with her what he had learned prior to her arrival? Do you think she expected that Adam would take even greater care of her than he did for all of the other animals? Yes.

We expect the one who loves us to be concerned with what is good and healthy for us. We expect to benefit in some way because we are married. Is this true for you? Have you grown less or more as a result of being married? Is your bank account richer? Is your affluence greater? Are you happier? Do you have more friends? What about your relationship with Jesus? Are you walking closer to Him? Are you reading his Word more often? Are you spending more time alone with Him in prayer and meditation?

Now, what about your impact upon your wife? How is being married to you working out for her? Would she say she has grown less or more as a result of being married to you? Is she richer? Does she have more affluence? Does she care about any of that? Is she happier? Does she have more friends? What about her relationship with Jesus? Is she walking closer to Him? Is she reading his Word more often than before? Is she spending more time with Him in prayer and meditation because of your encouragement or example?

God gave us our spouses to help us do what is right, to help us draw nearer to Him. We do not expect them to participate in our downfall. Yet, that is what the first couple did. They set an indelible pattern that most marriages still suffer from today. God's will for humankind back in the Garden was the same as it is now. We are to demonstrate the kind of love that rejoices in the truth—one that lovingly establishes God's Word as the authority in our homes. How can we become better at practicing love that rejoices in the truth?

In Genesis 4, Adam and Eve made peace with one another. Not only that, but they were once again in a right relationship with God. Subsequently, God's authority and Adam's leadership role was restored. This is good news: the first couple, though sinners, were once again obeying the rule and order God designed. In fact, it is evident that they passed onto Cain and Abel their knowledge of God:

> When she gave birth to Cain, she said, "With the Lord's help, I have produced a man!" Later she gave birth to his brother and named him Abel. When they grew up, Abel became a shepherd, while Cain cultivated the ground. When it was time for the harvest, Cain presented some of his crops as a gift to the Lord. Abel also brought a gift—the best portions of the firstborn lambs from his flock. (Genesis 4:1–4)

At this point the first family had returned to living under the rule of God. They recognized that God is the author of life (v.1). They sought to worship him. They were submissive to his will (vs 2–4). This brings us back to 1 Corinthians 13:6, "Love rejoices in the truth." John MacArthur explains, "The truth Paul is speaking about here is not simply factual truth. He is speaking of God's truth. God's revealed Word."[27] Love rejoices, not just in any truth, but in God's truth, His word, His commands, His design.

When God designed marriage, he established an order, a structure for how marriage was to run right. He assigned unique roles to the husband and wife. Adam was assigned the role of head of household and loving truth-keeper. Let's go to 1 Timothy 2 again momentarily. It reads in verse 13, "For it was Adam who was first created, and then Eve." This speaks of authority and responsibility, which, in the context of this verse, was established by the sequence of the creation of man. Adam was created first; hence, he was the first to know God. Adam was created first as the prototype for all who would follow. He was created first to establish his leadership and truth-protector role.

God equipped the man and the woman with certain characteristics for the roles he gave them. And he designed a structure in which the roles function best. This is the model we see in the first chapter of Genesis.

However, once the fall occurred, nothing is the way it is supposed to be. Lions are not playing gently with the lambs. Roses are not growing without thorns. Children are not naturally doing what is right. And husbands and wives are not automatically living happily ever after. Nothing is the way it is supposed to be since sin entered the world. Cornelius Plantinga Jr. in his book *Not the way it is supposed to be,* posits the idea that once sin entered the world, everything changed. He says, "Sin qualifies as the worst of our troubles because, among other things, it corrupts what is peculiarly human about us. Sin attaches to intention, memory, thought, speech, intelligent action—to all the special features of person-hood—and transforms them into weapons."[28]

Through Eve's and Adam's sin of mass destruction, marriage became distorted. Sin is destructive like that. For example, Sin perverts the beautiful act of love-making God designed especially for husband and wife and turns it into a weapon—one that destroys lives through the demeaning and dehumanizing violence of sexual abuse, sex slavery, sex trafficking, and pornography. Sin takes the beautiful image of the creator imprinted on marriage and turns it into the devilish and destructive mugshots of angry and vengeful divorcees. Sin corrupts the divine possibility of a husband as the avid student of God and loving teacher of his wife and turns him into a spiritually lazy, morally corrupt, emotionally absent wimp. Because of sin, guys, nothing is the way it is supposed to be.

Because of sin, men are often confused as to how they are supposed to act as husbands. Women are frustrated and feel they have to take the lead because their husbands refuse to do so. Children are confused why mom is always taking them to church while dad sits at home in front of the TV. Men are intimidated and inept at leading their wives in prayer. Parents are confused about what it means to be God's representatives lovingly disciplining their children. Marriages are in trouble because of the Fall. All of this is because Adam failed to be the preserver of Truth in his marriage.

God, in full knowledge of Eve's characteristics, presented her to Adam. He introduced her to Adam and not the other way around. In doing this, God meant for the woman to see her man in a certain light…to see him as God's representative. Think about this:

- To what degree does your wife see you as God's representative in your home?
- What occasion do you give her to see you as such?
- Are you the leader when it comes to prayer, Bible study, or repentance?
- Are you the man who rejoices in the truth in your marriage?

Guys, I am going to come right out and say it: God holds us responsible to have enough knowledge of God's truth to help our wife grow in her knowledge of Him. Of course, you cannot force her to know God. You cannot force her to believe in God. However, you are responsible that she knows about God—and not because you lord it over her or shout it at her in an argument. She knows him because you, by example, love her enough to "rejoice in the truth."

CHAPTER 10

Love Steps Up
Rather than Backing Down

I n the previous chapters, we saw who Adam was before and after the Fall. Adam was God's idea, his concept. God designed Man to consist of body, mind, and soul. Adam would look different from other animals. He would have mental capacity that other animals lack. He would be able to reflect, analyze, and alter his own behavior. He would have a conscience. He would have the power of choice. God also gave specific characteristics to the male versus the female human. He gave male body parts to Adam and female body parts to Eve. He made the male physically stronger than the female. Most importantly to us as Christian husbands, Adam was designed to be protector, provider, and priest in his marriage. He was given unique, even additional, responsibilities above those which Eve was given.

Do you get the sense that I am hinting that husbands are held accountable by God in a special way for their wives? Absolutely. In fact, this is why Adam's sin was so grievous. Scripture puts it this way, "As by one man, Adam, sin entered the world..." That's right—Adam, more than Eve, is responsible for things not being the way they are supposed to be. Both were equally guilty of sin. However, when it comes to accountability, God evidently shows us whom he held more accountable for the spiritual health of their marriage.

In Genesis right after Adam and Eve sinned and hid themselves, God walked in the Garden knowing fullwell what had occurred (Genesis 3:8–9). Who does He call into account? Does He call both Adam and Eve? Or more specifically, since he knew Eve was the one talking with the Serpent and ate the fruit first, did he call her out? No. He called upon Adam and proceeded to confront him with the transgression. Now hear this: God is holding you and me accountable because he has given us a unique capacity and need to protect women, to be vigilant in minimizing and preventing threat to our wives.

You know the feeling you get in your gut as a man when someone does something to offend the woman you love? Or the compelling need to intervene if you were to see a man beating on a woman? Or should you find out that your sister's boyfriend is cheating on her with multiple girlfriends? This instinct comes from how God made you—with the natural desire and propensity to protect and defend your wife against danger and evil. First Corinthians 13:7 describes love as always protecting. Paul uses the Greek word *stegō*, which means "to cover closely, to protect."[29] It speaks of the type of love that fosters unwavering commitment to someone. Husbands who love their wives are committed to protecting them. John MacArthur writes, "Love bears all things by protecting others from exposure, ridicule, or harm. Even when sin is certain, love tries to correct it with the least possible hurt and harm to the guilty person. Love never protects sin but is anxious to protect the sinner."[30]

But something went wrong with Adam. He denied who God had made him to be. And that was the gravest part of his sin—denying the very essence of what God had put in him, which was to lovingly keep Eve safe, to protect her against evil. God told Adam about the evil that would be unleashed once the fruit was eaten before He presented Eve to him. And in doing this, He equipped Adam with the knowledge he needed in order to keep Eve safe.

Sadly, too many of us are guilty of Adam's 'not-loving' behavior—having a wavering, flimsy commitment. When a threat arises, we crumble quickly. When temptation looms, we yield without resisting. When the opportunity arises for us to condemn sin, we remain silent. Too often we are the ones allowing the evil one access and free range. Or worse, our lack of commitment to holiness and fidelity has us bringing evil into our marriages. But God is calling us out. He is marshaling obedient and committed Christian men to stand in the gap for Him and for our wives. He is calling us to live out 1 Corinthians 13:7. Love always protects—it steps up when there is danger. Are you ready to be that man, that husband, that obedient Adam, the protector, the committed man God is requiring you to be? If so, here is how this type of loving commitment looks.

Husbands who are committed to loving their wives put aside self-interest for the benefit of their wives. They sacrifice for her. They see such sacrifices more as helpful to their marriage rather than harmful to themselves. 'Love always protects' conveys a commitment to defend our wives—to preserve her comfort and safety. Love fuels an enduring and unwavering commitment.

Commitment, in fact, is one of the key contributors to success in marriage. Commitment manifests in one of two ways: in the dedication a person demonstrates toward their spouse, or in the constraints a person enforces upon themselves for the benefit of their spouse. For example, dedication shows up in how likely you are to rearrange your schedule in order to spend time doing something your wife likes to do. This may not seem like a big deal to you, but research by Rusbult shows that when you take the initiative to prioritize something that is important to your wife, you enhance the durability of your marriage.

Dedication is measured by how much I *want to do* for my wife, not in what I feel I am *obligated to* do. For instance, a dedicated husband will do things like setting aside regular and consistent time to talk with his wife about the book she is reading or the project she is working on. What about you, husband: are you dedicated to your wife? Are you dedicated to such a degree that you prioritize her needs over your own?

Constraint on the other hand is what I deny myself because of my commitment to my wife. It begs the question: "What am I willing to not do; where am I willing to not go; who am I willing to not see, because I love my wife?" In chapter 2, I talked about the discussions we usually have with hurting couples. I talked about how we often ask the following rhetorical questions to illustrate a point:

"Do you love your wife enough to give up alcohol? Do you love her enough to give up pornography? Do you love her enough to stop drinking in other women? Do you love her enough to look to the other side of the road where the female is not jogging?" The unspoken, expected, and likely answer is, "Yes." However, reality sets in when we follow up with this question: "So why don't you? Why don't you give up the behaviors that are hurting your wife and destroying your marriage and testimony?" This is what constraint consists of: it is the restrictions I put upon myself in order to lovingly protect my wife and marriage.

Dedication addresses the "I want to" aspect of a relationship. Constraint addresses the "I have to" aspect. Dedication is what you voluntarily invest, whereas constraint is what you feel is morally required of you to do. Dedication pushes you to take action—you are motivated to serve and honor her. Constraint, on the other hand, pulls you into action—it causes you to devalue, denounce, and disallow alluring alternatives. Commitment looks like this: I am dedicated to my wife. Hence, I double check the door locks at night, and I guard my heart against lust during the day. Commitment also looks like this: I constrain myself. I stop doing certain things. For instance, I do not respond to the text from an ex-girl-friend, and I put software on my computer to prevent visits to pornographic sites.

Love that always protects demonstrates that your wife is the most important person to you. She can rely upon you to always be there, exclusively, for her. She knows that you are committed to her.

Earlier on, we learned that when we are romancing our wives, we are in hot pursuit of them. We are trying very hard to get them to trust us, to enable them to give their love to us. We are doing things for them so they may know that we are sincere. We are trying to woo them, win them over, and they know it. We are giving them reasons to believe us. Romance is like that. It is warm, endearing, inviting, and safe. Romance by its very nature makes this type of promise. It says, "I love you. You can depend upon me. I am committed to you. I will protect you."

Love, Guaranteed!

This is the kind of implied promise Adam made in Genesis 2. Adam said to Eve the moment he met her: "This is bone of my bones, and flesh of my flesh" (Genesis 2:23). Adam plants this idea in Eve's head, "Eve you are the one . . . the only one. We are one. We are a unit. We are a special event. We are different from all the others. Our union is unique and special above the rest, put together by God—an unbreakable covenant. In me you have love, guaranteed."

Doesn't this sound familiar? Doesn't this sound like the guarantee we may hear at a wedding? Let's for a moment just imagine we are at Adam and Eve's wedding ceremony. We are about to hear the exchange of vows between the man and his wife. "Dearly beloved we are gathered here today in the sight of God to join this man and this woman together in Holy matrimony. Adam, do you take Eve as your wife, to have and to hold." But wait, right here the vows are different from the vows we say today . . . today our vows go onto say, "From this day forward, in sickness and in health, for richer, for poorer, as long as you both shall live." But in the Garden, the vows would have said, "Adam do you take Eve as your wife, to have and to hold, *without sickness* and *without death*, as you live together forever?" That's what they had— an everlasting bond—love, guaranteed. They were happily stuck together, forever. And take note of this: They-Were-Safe. Safe in God's presence. Safe in the Garden. Safe in God's love. Safe in each other's love. Safe and secure in one another.

This is what we see in the second part of Genesis 2:23, when Adam proclaims, "She shall be called woman for she was taken out of man." Adam asserts that he and Eve are a couple, and at the same time, he establishes that even though they are one, they are also two distinct people. This is a very important biblical truth. Husbands and wives are made one by the sacrament of marriage as we read in Genesis 2:24. We are a unit—a family in God's eyes. We are one in sexual intimacy. We are one in spiritual intimacy—we are to share the same faith and have a devotion to God that is greater than our devotion to anyone else. We are one in emotional intimacy—our attachment to each other is to be the strongest and most exclusive relationship we have with another human being.

We are to be the earthly safe haven for our wives. God calls us and equips us to step up, not back down. We are to be the safest person on earth for her, to be her safe haven, the person she turns to sexually, emotionally, and spiritually. As a husband, I am to have unfailing commitment to her. I am to demonstrate that love is not fleeting, merely a feeling. Nor is it blissfulness, but rather, it is the willingness to endure hardship, to stay in the fight against evil for her. It is the recurring pursuit of maintaining connection with her. Thus, even when I feel unloved, when my wants or needs are being denied or unmet, I am to guard my heart, purify my thoughts, and restrain my eyes.

Paul Tripp says in moments like this, we can call upon Jesus to deliver us not from our spouse, but rescue us from our self. Love is surrendering to painful self-sacrifice. Adam's problem was not "the woman," as he complained to God. The problem in the Garden for Adam was Adam. The problem with Adam was the man that he allowed himself to become. In that moment of temptation, it became clear that he was no longer surrendered to the control of God. "Self" had taken control.

Brothers, these moments of our lives reveal who is sitting on the throne of our hearts. Jesus died for the difficult and trying moments with my wife. He died to help me with my 'here and now,' as Paul Tripp would say. He died that I may no longer live for myself but instead live for Him. He designed me to be this kind of man. He is my Safe haven. And when I live consciously for Him, as it says in 2 Corinthians 5:15, "Christ died that we who have received His new life, no longer live for ourselves but instead we live for Christ who died and was raised for me." When He is enthroned, I am equipped to be fully and faithfully committed to my wife. Then, I am empowered to unfailingly love and protect my wife.

CHAPTER II

Love is Permanent Rather than Transient

"Love always trusts, hopes and perseveres." These exciting words in 1 Corinthians 13:7 are summarized in verse 8: "Love never ends." What a wonderful promise. The Greek word for perseveres, *hupomenō*, means to remain steadfast in the face of unpleasant circumstances.[31] Love does not give up. The Greek concept for 'never ends,' *piptō*, means to resist and succeed at not being beaten down. Love is long lasting, durable, persistent, and resilient.

Love gets up from a fall; it rebounds after heart break. It is the broken-hearted prodigal son's father never giving up hope, never ceasing to love—enduringly loving day after day looking to the horizon for his son to return, then throwing a party when he does. Love works against not trusting, not hoping, not persisting. That is the picture of love in Ephesians 5:25. Christ's love for his people endures; it is not wavering; it is permanent. One way to say this is love works hard. It is not lazy or laid back.

In the same way, the Christian husband's love is to be hard-working, durable, persistent, enduring, unwavering and without condition—guaranteed. Ephesians 5:25 does not say, husbands love your wife if she remains a certain size or is sexy in bed or stays forever young or is pleasant all the time. No, none of that—we are to love unconditionally, consistently. So how does God expect us to do that? How do we make love last?

New and mature couples ask these questions all the time. They want to know how to keep the fire burning in their marriages. Couples in deep distress ask these questions also. The sincere and God-fearing spouse desperately wants to save their marriage. That is why a few years ago, I set out to find answers to help couples restore lost love and trust. My dissertation topic was, "How does ministry impact romance and attachment?" I interviewed couples who seemed to have cultivated healthy, long-lasting, fruitful marriages. One of the questions I asked couples was, "How do you keep romance going in your marriage?" Here is what they said. This list can help you assess your own marriage. Are these true of you?

- **I prioritize time with my spouse.** The spouses had a desire to and made time to spend with their spouse. They enjoyed being in each other's presence.
- **I retreat to my spouse** as a safe haven when threatened or in need of comfort. When things go wrong in life, they seek their spouse first and above all other humans as a refuge, a safe place.
- **I depend upon my spouse as a secure base** from which to explore the world. When taking on new challenges or when about to make a major decision, the couples relied upon their spouse's input and support.
- **I experience separation distress** when my spouse is not responsive or inaccessible when needed. They miss their spouse when they are away from them beyond their normal schedule. They feel a sense of loss when physically or emotionally distanced from their spouse.

- **I yearn for intimate, caring, and satisfying lovemaking** with my spouse. They have an established frequency and behaviors for lovemaking which are mutually observed and protected.
- **I cultivate spiritual intimacy** with my spouse. They center their relationship in their own quiet time of Bible reading and prayer. They are confident in theirs and their spouse's individual relationship with Jesus Christ.
- **I challenge the unspoken.** They do not allow important discussions or concerns to go unaddressed. They create a safe space for any topic, especially the difficult ones to be discussed.

Romance, as illustrated in the list of 'must do's' above, requires hard work. Enduring love requires effort. Some of that effort requires us to look at the types of expectations we brought with us when we decided to get married. What did you expect of your spouse?

You might have expected them to make you happy or be fun to live with. Maybe you were looking for someone to do ministry with or who would help you grow in your walk with Christ. But one obvious expectation usually goes unmentioned. We expect romance. We expect the chase of romance and the surrender to it.

We expect foreplay. We expect intimate touch. We expect focused, undivided, and passion-driven attention. We expect to make love. We expect to enjoy one another. We expect mutual satisfaction. For this to be the case, however, we need to experience prevailing togetherness.

We need to have long periods of unbroken oneness. We need extended periods when we have more loving behavior than 'not loving' behavior. How long has it been since you had a fight? How did the fight impact your lovemaking? How often do you fight? Your answers reveal whether or not your love life is healthy.

Caryl Rusbult explains how such "diagnostic situations" arise and reveal the health of our relationships.[32] These situations, she suggests, usually begin with a spouse's bad behavior, inconsideration, or irritation. However, these acts provide an opportunity for the innocent spouse to resist the impulse to retaliate and instead respond in an understanding and patient way, as 1 Corinthians 13 instructs, "love is patient, long suffering and tender hearted." The more obedient to God each spouse is, the healthier the relationship is likely to be. Therefore, the more likely it is for the couple to quickly get back to loving each other freely again. The spouses in my dissertation study gave examples of how they successfully got back to a lovemaking mindset:

- They did not allow the behavior of their spouse to cause them to misbehave in return.
- They did not view the 'not loving behavior' of their spouse as permanent or unchangeable. Instead of arguing, they chose to pray silently.
- They looked for a moment to reach out and touch their spouse with a hug, holding their hand, or a kiss.
- They gently changed the subject, knowing there would be a less emotional time when they could discuss the topic later.
- They looked for ways to continue or return to the intimacy they had before the misbehavior. This was especially important when spontaneous conversation and interaction ceased.

As you can see, the couples in the study took a firm stand on committing to remain loving to each other, despite a misbehaving spouse.

So, when our spouse does wrong, how do we continue to romance? How can we go on loving? Leslie Verneck in her book, *How to Act Right When Your Spouse Acts Wrong*, writes:

> Most of us acknowledge that there are no perfect marriages or perfect spouses. We know that having a good marriage requires effort and

hard work. At times, however, in the midst of that pain and struggle we can lose sight of what marriage is all about. We forget that we have made a covenant promise to love for better or worse. In the better times, love is usually easy. When worse comes, we often don't know how to continue to love when we are angry, hurt, scared, or don't feel very loving.[33]

The hard times, when our spouse does wrong, are when we need to remember that love really is love only when it is enduring and durable. Sometimes to continue to love can be painfully hard to do. That is why marriage is not to be entered into lightly.

MARRIAGE DEMANDS MORE THAN HUMANS CAN GIVE; SUCCESS REQUIRES DIVINE INTERVENTION AND SUBMISSION TO GOD.

Marriage is quite a miraculous event. God designed it to be unique among all human relationships. Our marriage is *our* marriage—a one-of-a-kind union—to the one person made especially for us. Usually, we marry someone who, at one time, was a perfect stranger, totally unknown to us. Quite unexpectedly, they became the love of our life, the apple of our eye, the sunshine in our days. This deep level of emotional investment multiplies the hurt when we betray or offend one another. This is why, I am pleading that you, husband, would seek God's face, asking him to increase your love and your lovingness toward your wife. I pray the same for myself. May we become known for our enduring love for our wives.

Here are five ideas to help us practically show our undying love for our wives:

1. **Practice 'we-ness' in your marriage.** What you do or fail to do directly impacts your wife. Be mindful of Hebrews 11:1 that speaks of laying aside the encumbrance that holds us back. What weighs you down weighs her down. Therefore, we should be careful to love God and her in a way to spur her on to love and good works (Hebrews 10:24). Affirm your identity as her husband. You belong to her, and she belongs to you. In God's eyes you are one. Do more of what creates a loving environment in your home. Do things for her. If you do not normally cook, cook. If you do not often clean the bathrooms, clean them. If you do not get up at 2 am when the child is crying, get up. Do things to her. Learn afresh how to give her the type of intimate care she craves. For some

women, this is non-sexual touching. For others, this is frequent and passionate lovemaking. Romance her.

2. **Be God's pacesetter in your marriage.** You set the pace and depth of spiritual growth in your marriage. Brothers, how you live for Christ in your marriage matters for all eternity. John Piper explains the role of the man in his home: "Men, no one influences the spiritual climate of our homes like we do. If we are lukewarm and careless, we send a spiritual draft throughout the household. If we burn as a furnace for the Lord, even the most antagonistic child within our walls will feel the warming influence. Our great aim is to lead our families in a way worthy of God. Why else are they put under our care? To help us think through how to do this, I believe it helpful to borrow from the classic categories applied to Christ: *prophet, priest, and king.* We are prophets who speak the word over our households; priests who give ourselves to intercessory prayer, speaking to God on behalf of our loved ones; and kings who govern, defend, and provide for them."³⁴ Brothers, in this way, be her guide; love and care for her by walking near to God. Romance her.

3. **Maintain an undefiled marriage bed.** Sex and sexual perversion are prevalent today. Tantalizing sexual acts are in almost every movie, in sitcoms, and in overheard conversations at work. If we are not on our guard, we can be exposed to a steady stream of permissive and promiscuous sex. According to Cutrer and Glahn, in their book, *Sexual Intimacy in Marriage*, by the age of 19, 64 percent of males in the United States are already sexually active.[35] That being the case, most of us do not come into marriage as virgins. Thus, it is highly likely that most of us come to marriage with indelibly imprinted memories of our past sexual experiences. I encourage you brothers, keep sex with you wife pure. Leave your past in the past. Do not bring images of anyone other than your wife into your lovemaking. Fill your mind with her love, her fragrance, and her touch. Romance her.

4. **Demonstrate confidence in God's power in your marriage.** Joshua in the Old Testament loved his wife and family. We can observe how much Joshua loved them because of what he modeled. He demonstrated his confidence in God to his family and to his nation in this declaration: "And if it seems evil unto you to serve

the Lord, choose you this day whom ye will serve; but as for me and my house, we will serve the Lord" (Joshua 24:15). In committing to leading his family in this way, he showed that he loved them. Brothers, look for opportunities to show your confidence in God. Let your faith be demonstrated in your words and deeds. Joshua was that type of man. By God's grace, we can be the same.

5. **Look for God's hand in life's events.** Marriage is a life-changing event. No other event exposes us to as many relationship challenges as marriage. Through marriage we inherit another set of parents, siblings, and family culture. Through marriage we get to know another person on a deeper level than we could from other relationships. Through marriage, if allowed, God will make us into who he means for us to be. In our marriage God is likely to use many of the most challenging life events to conform us to his image. We can recognize these God events, David Powlison says, by three common features:

1) You are struggling with a challenging, troubling, disorienting situation, which presents a sense of personal struggle with sins, disturbing emotions, or confusion.

2) You observe God's intervening voice and hand, via Scripture, often mediated through a godly person.

3) You can look back at the end and see the way all these came together, by the grace of God, in a noticeable and remarkable change in your faith, obedience, and circumstances.[36]

This is what I experienced. At the height of my resentment when all I wanted was to divorce my wife, God used His word and a godly person, Judy, to lovingly confront me with my sin, which resulted in my repentance and our renewal as a couple. We refer to this remarkable event as the best worse thing that ever happened to us. We needed a new marriage; our old one was built on the wrong foundation. Jesus was there in our crisis, drawing us to Himself—inviting us to surrender (Revelation 3:20). He will be there for you, or as the case may be, is with you right now in your crisis. If your marriage is in trouble, know that He is right there in your midst, inviting you to yield to him. Trust him and make him Lord and Master of your life and marriage. Let him transform how you care for and romance your wife.

CHAPTER 12

Reimagine Loving Rather than 'Not Loving'

Mitch and Mary fell in love quickly. He was an up-and-coming executive for a professional sports team, and she was an executive for a luxury car company. They were the consummate power couple

Another couple, Eddie and Lucy, were high school sweethearts. Eddie recounts how he spotted her across a football field one day and decided then that he would marry her. The problem was, she had a boyfriend.

However, Eddie devised a solution to that problem. He would tutor her boyfriend in mathematics and keep a close eye on any fissure that developed in their relationship. His plan worked. By the time they graduated from college, Eddie and Lucy had already checked off three of life's most significant milestones. Eddie had his engineering degree and his first job as a professional. He and Lucy had their marriage certificate, and as proud parents, they had the birth certificate of their newborn son.

A third couple, Sean and Gem, had a good marriage, a good home, and a stable family life—until Gem found herself resenting Sean. More and more, she began feeling that she was unimportant to him. His work and his career were all that mattered to him. Not only that, but she also felt that for a very long time, regardless of how she pleaded with him, he was not willing to take the lead spiritually in their marriage.

Mitch and Mary, Eddie and Lucy, Sean and Gem, and Judy and I have two things in common. The first one is, we had marriages that faced divorce.

Mitch and Mary's path to divorce was fueled by the very thing that made them successful: their work ethic and love for their jobs. After five years, they decided to end what had become a non-communicative, unloving, and painful relationship.

Eddie and Lucy, within the first five years of their marriage, experienced several life-changing events that led them to divorce court. One event was Eddie's new-found faith in Jesus Christ. Lucy wanted no part of it. Eddie wanted and pursued an even deeper relationship with Christ. However, Lucy's lifestyle and behavior was increasingly juxtaposed to Eddie's new faith. Eventually, they agreed to file for divorce.

Sean was surprised when Gem brought up the idea of divorce. After all, they had many of the things couples hoped for. They had the cars, the houses: one in the city and one on the beach. They had respectful children who were doing well in their careers. What else could they ask for? Yet that was not enough. Gem told us that her heart was cold and numb towards her husband. She was ready to quit, and though she felt divorce was a sin, she was finding it more and more alluring.

The second thing we had in common was all four couples came eventually to understand how Christ died to reverse the impact of Adam's sin upon our marriages. We do not have to suffer divorce. We do not have to commit adultery. We do not have to look at pornography. We do not have to settle for being a roommate in a loveless marriage. We do not need to let resentment grow. We do not need to fail to keep the greatest promise we can make to another human.

We, YOU, can choose otherwise. Christian husbands and wives can choose to love. We can choose to reconnect. We can choose to reclaim our marriage. We can choose to reignite, revive, and renew unhealthy, dying, or even dead love. We can choose to love like Christ.

We claim to "love" all the time. We date, fall in love, fall out of love, break up, ghost one another, and move on again and again. We, in essence, practice breaking up for years before we get married. In a sense, we rehearse divorce. We choose whom we love and for how long. Too often, however, lust, infatuation, and emotional neediness are misinterpreted as love. We talk about falling in love, but we don't really, do we? What happens when you suffer a fall? A mishap—falling is an accident; loving is not—we choose to love.

GOD'S LOVE FOR US WAS NOT HAPHAZARD; HE CHOSE TO LOVE US (EPHESIANS 1:4).

To love someone requires a conscious act. We allow ourselves to love someone. That is why grace is so amazing…God chooses to love sinners: me, you, and our wives. He does not do it by accident. And, because Jesus loved us enough to die for us, we can love too.

Sadly, Mitch and Mary, Eddie and Lucy, Sean and Gem, and Judy and I discovered this truth the hard way. All of us experienced the pain and devastation that 'not loving' brings. Mitch and Mary ended their marriage. However, unbeknownst to each other, they individually surrendered control of their lives to Jesus and His teaching. After five years of being divorced, tragedy struck Mary's family. Mitch heard of the tragedy and reached out to Mary with condolences. That gesture was significant in that it led them to talk about the possibility of dating again. They did. But they realized that they had gone about their first relationship the wrong way, built on the wrong premise. This time, they committed to non-sexual dating, Christian pre-marital counseling, and a Christ-centered lifestyle. Judy and I knew them during their divorce, and we are so happy to know them as happily remarried now for seven years.

Eddie and Lucy were in a very bad place at the time of their divorce hearing. Without his knowledge, Lucy had discovered credit cards during the early days of their marriage. Eddie, an engineer with a very successful company, had great credit. Lucy reveled in his success—so much so, that she applied for, got approved for, and maxed out twenty credit cards without Eddie's knowledge. As result, Eddie was forced to file for bankruptcy. However, a few days before the divorce was final, Lucy called Eddie to say she wanted to come back home. She wanted her family again.

Eddie told us that he accepted her request only because he felt it was his duty as a Christian. They both remembered exactly what he told her in response: "You can come back. But I do not love you and I do not trust you." They also recounted how their 3-year-old son responded when Eddie told him his mother was coming home. He said, "Oh daddy, mommy will hurt you again." That was fifty-one years ago. Eddie and Lucy are loving, insightful, and highly effective marriage mentors for struggling couples today.

Providentially, God had a plan for Gem and Sean beyond what they realized. He had a way for them to reimagine loving and caring for each other. It involved something that went painfully against what Sean's culture taught him: he had to confess that he had failed. Gem also had to come face-to-face with a reality that she had suppressed. She had to own that part of her hurt and resentment toward Sean was directly connected to the unprocessed, unforgiven sexual abuse she suffered at the hands of her father. By God's grace, they both found healing and renewal through confession and repentance.

This is what God does. In fact, this is what *only God* can do. The other couples, and Judy and I, came to the darkest, most hopeless time in marriage when, in our minds, our marriage was over. We believed our relationship to be irretrievable. We were not in love. Staying together was not in our minds, nor was it our desire. And yet, in this season, the impossible happened—by God's grace, we began to reimagine loving our spouses.

Husbands hear this, God's grace brought me, Judy, and the other spouses to reimagine passionate, caring, forgiving, kind love for each other. Only God changes hearts. He alone brings beauty out of ashes. He alone can raise the dead. He alone has the power to reverse the curse of Adam. His enduring, divine, steadfast, guaranteed love enables us to reimagine loving our spouse. In him, love has no bounds, no limits. In Him, we have love, guaranteed (Lamentations 3:22–23).

WE CAN GIVE OUR SPOUSE WHAT THEY REALLY WANT: OUR GUARANTEED LOVE.

Imagine that. As Christians, we have the capacity to love like Jesus. We too, because of His love in us, can dare to guarantee love to our spouse. We can keep on loving. Let's rejoice in serving him this way in our marriage. Be His representative. Be the standard bearer of love. Make it so your spouse knows that they have your love, guaranteed.

For the Christian husband, walking worthy involves three behaviors: loving your wife like Christ loves the Church (Ephesians 5:25), loving your wife in a way that helps her grow in holiness (5:27), and loving your wife like your own body (5:28). Scripture provides the context and instruction for how we should reframe our thinking, revamp our loving, and reinvigorate our passion for our wives. These two ideas capture the purpose for this book. My desire is that our love for our wives would be so complete, so observable, and so impactful that it will result in a level of intimacy, passion, faithfulness, and love far beyond what we ever thought possible. I pray that our spouses will come to experience with us love that is unwavering, one that never ends.

In 1 Corinthians 13:3, we find these words: "If I speak with the tongues of men, and of angels and have not love, I have become as a noisy gong and clanging cymbal."

Paul uses the image of off-beat, out-of-tune, musical instruments—noisy gongs and clashing cymbals—to describe what it is like to perform good, even great things without love. We can have a marriage devoid of love where conversations are like the irritating "sound of noisy gongs and clanging cymbals" (1 Corinthians 13:1). Or we can have marriages where the intimacy, caring, and self-sacrificial love is like that of Christ's love for the church. The difference boils down to the choices each spouse makes. We choose to foster health in our marriage. We choose whether we prioritize our marriage. We choose to reflect Christ in our marriage. We choose to allow our marriage to tell the story of his redemptive power. Or we choose to leave Christ out of our marriage. I pray that you make the choice to exult Jesus—that you choose to love, to connect, or to reconnect to Him as your loving role model. I pray that you allow the Holy Spirit to inspire you to reimagine loving your spouse. And I pray that as a result, you and your spouse will grow and stay together for a lifetime in love, guaranteed.

APPENDIX A

Love, Guaranteed: Date Night and Workday

U se this QR code to find out more about Love, Guaranteed marriage events in Washington, D.C. and access FREE Healthy Marriage and Conversation Impact surveys.

Questions to Guide Your 8-Week Journey

To help you begin your journey toward loving your spouse in earnest, feel free to use the following eight weeks of guided questions and prayers:

ASSIGNMENT WEEK 1: *Getting to know your spouse's interests.*

1. What does your spouse yearn to learn, do more of, or become?
2. When is a good time to casually chat together about this?
3. How can you serve your spouse in this area?

PRAY: ASK GOD TO INCREASE YOUR ABILITY TO LIVE PHILLIPIANS 2:3-5

ASSIGNMENT WEEK 2: *Getting to know your spouse's unique needs.*

1. How are you praying for God to provide for your spouse?
2. How does your spouse let you know what they need from you?
3. What need does your spouse regularly pray for?

PRAY: ASK GOD TO HELP MAKE GALATIANS 5:13 REAL
AS YOU LISTEN CAREFULLY THIS WEEK FOR YOUR SPOUSE'S NEEDS

ASSIGNMENT WEEK 3: *Getting to know how your spouse wants to and needs to spend time with you.*

1. Ask your spouse what he/she considers to be your "special times" together?
2. Does your spouse feel you are spending time with them in the way they want and need you to?
3. If so, what does that look like? If not, why not?

PRAY: ASK GOD TO HELP YOU AND YOUR SPOUSE RESPOND WITH HUMILITY AND GRACE AS COLOSSIANS 4:6 TEACHES.

ASSIGNMENT WEEK 4: *Creating an increasing level of excitement in your marriage.*

1. Other than sex, what does your spouse find exciting?
2. What small, daily thing can you start doing that pleases your spouse?
3. What change over the next seven days in your behavior would be both pleasing and surprising to your spouse?

PRAY: ASK GOD TO SHOW YOU HOW TO BE MORE PLEASING IN AN EPHESIANS 5:33 WAY TO YOUR SPOUSE

ASSIGNMENT WEEK 5: *Creating meaningful experiences with your spouse.*

1. What is your mission as a couple?
2. Who benefits from the goals you are pursuing as a couple?
3. Other than in your own family, or ministry, how are you sharing the love of Christ as a couple?

*PRAY: ASK GOD TO REVEAL TO YOU, HOW HE WANTS YOU
AS A COUPLE TO DEMONSTRATE JAMES 1:27*

ASSIGNMENT WEEK 6: *Improving your gentleness with each other.*

1. What would improved gentleness toward your spouse look like?
2. How can you help your spouse be gentler with you?
3. What words, remarks, or sarcasm do you need to stop immediately in order to start being gentler?

*PRAY: ASK GOD TO HELP YOU MEMORIZE AND
PRACTICE COLOSSIANS 3:12,13.*

ASSIGNMENT WEEK 7: *Increasing the atmosphere of transparency in your marriage.*

1. Confess to your spouse what causes you to withdraw or shut them out.
2. Discuss what it would look like to keep a zero balance and full tank.
3. Rearrange your time, so you are able to get up in the morning to pray together at the beginning of the day for the next 21 days.

PRAY: ASK GOD TO HELP YOU MEMORIZE AND PRACTICE GALATIANS 6:1

ASSIGNMENT WEEK 8: *increasing romance in your marriage.*

1. Do you know when your spouse feels most connected to you? Ask them now.
2. Do you know for sure what puts your spouse in the "mood"? Check with them to be sure.
3. For each of the next three weeks, design a romantic evening together. However, husbands, remember, allow for touching that does not have to lead to sex.

PRAY: ASK GOD TO HELP YOU YEARN FOR YOUR SPOUSE IN A SONG OF SOLOMON CHAPTER 5:1-5 WAY.

About the Authors

D r. and Mrs. Tucker are directors of a marriage ministry, providing prayer and counseling to more than one thousand couples who have encountered all sorts of challenges in their marriages. Dr. Ken Tucker holds a Doctor of Educational Ministry degree from Dallas Theological Seminary focusing on Relationship Science. Mrs. Tucker has a Masters in

Elementary School Counseling. Dr. Tucker has written six books related to leadership. They currently reside in Arlington, Virginia.

Bibliography

Burton, Neel. "The Lost Virtue of Patience How Patience Is Being Eroded, and Why It Still Matters." *Psychology Today*, 2019. Accessed March 7, 2023. https://www.psychologytoday.com/intl/blog/hide-and-seek/201908/the-lost-virtue-patience.

Cutrer William, Sandra L. Glahn, and Michael Sytsma. *Sexual Intimacy in Marriage*. Grand Rapids, MI: Kregel Publications, 2020.

Evans, Tony. *The Tony Evans Bible Commentary*. Nashville TN: Hollman Bible Publishers, 2019.

Gottman, John Mordechai. *The Marriage Clinic: A Scientifically Based Marital Therapy.* New York: W.W. Norton & Co, 1999.

Harley, Willard F. *His Needs, Her Needs.* Grand Rapids, MI: Baker Publishing Group, 2022.

MacArthur, John. *1 Corinthians, MacArthur New Testament Commentary.* Chicago, IL: Moody, 1984.

MacArthur, John. *Ephesians, MacArthur New Testament Commentary.* Chicago, IL: The Moody Bible Institute, 1986.

Morse, Greg. "Prophet, Priest, and King the High Calling of Christian." *Desiring God,* April 30, 2021. Accessed March 3, 2023. https://www.desiringgod.org/articles/prophet-priest-and-king.

Plantinga, Cornelius Jr. *Not the Way It's Supposed to Be: A Breviary of Sin.* Grand Rapids, MI: Eerdmans, 1996.

Powlison, David. "How Does Scripture Change You?" *Journal of Biblical Counseling* 26, no. 2 (2012): 26.

Robertson, Archibald, and Alfred Plummer. *A Critical and Exegetical Commentary on the First Epistle of St. Paul to the Corinthians.* International Critical Commentary. New York: T. & T. Clark, 1911.

Rusbult, Caryl E., and Paul A. M. van Lange. "Interdependence, Interactions and Relationships." *Annual Reviews* (2003): 363.

Smalley, Gary, and John Trent. *The Two Sides of Love: The Secret to Valuing Differences*. Carol Stream, IL: Tyndale House, 2019.

Spiegel, James S. "How to Be Good in a World Gone Bad." *Christianity Today*, 2023. Accessed March 23, 2023. https://www.christianitytoday.com/biblestudies/articles/spiritualformation/virtue-of-patience.html.

Stanley, Scott, Daniel Trathen, Savanna McCain and Milt Bryan. *A Lasting Promise: The Christian Guide to Fighting for Your Marriage*. San Francisco: Jossey-Bass, 2014.

Tripp, Paul David. *Instruments in the Redeemer's Hand People in Need of Change Helping People in Need of Change*. Phillipsburg, NJ: P&R Publishing Company, 2002.

Vernick Leslie, *How to Act Right When Your Spouse Acts Wrong*: *Indispensable Guides for Godly Living*. New York: Crown Publishing, 2001. Kindle Edition.

Walvoord John F. and Roy B. Zuck. *The Bible Knowledge Commentary*. Wheaton IL: Victor Books, 1983.

Wiersbe, Warren W. *The Wiersbe Bible Commentary: The New Testament*. Colorado Springs, CO: David C. Cook, 2007.

Yates, Henry. "The Story behind the Song: I Want to Know What Love Is by Foreigner." *Classic Rock*, February 1, 2022. Accessed February 20, 2023. https://www.loudersound.com/features/the-story-behind-the-song-i-want-to-know-what-love-is-by-foreigner.

Endnotes

1 Henry Yates, "The Story behind the Song: I Want to Know What Love Is by Foreigner," Classic Rock, February 1, 2022, accessed February 20, 2023, https://www.loudersound.com/features/the-story-behind-the-song-i-want-to-know-what-love-is-by-foreigner.

2 John MacArthur, Ephesians, MacArthur New Testament Commentary (Chicago, IL: The Moody Bible Institute, 1986), 273.

3 Unless otherwise noted, The Holy Bible, English Standard Version will be used.

4   John Mordechai Gottman, The Marriage Clinic: A Scientifically Based Marital Therapy (New York: W.W. Norton & Co, 1999), 12.

5   Archibald Robertson and Alfred Plummer, A Critical and Exegetical Commentary on the First Epistle of St. Paul to the Corinthians, International Critical Commentary (New York: T. & T. Clark, 1911), 286.

6   John MacArthur, 1 Corinthians, MacArthur New Testament Commentary (Chicago, IL: Moody, 1984), 338.

7   Neel Burton, "The Lost Virtue of Patience How Patience Is Being Eroded, and Why It Still Matters," Psychology Today, 2019, accessed March 7, 2023, https://www.psychologytoday.com/intl/blog/hide-and-seek/201908/the-lost-virtue-patience.

8   James S. Spiegel, "How to Be Good in a World Gone Bad," Christianity Today, 2023, accessed March 23, 2023, https://www.christianitytoday.com/biblestudies/articles/spiritualformation/virtue-of-patience.html.

9   James S. Spiegel, "How to Be Good in a World Gone Bad," Christianity Today, 2023, accessed March 23, 2023, https://www.christianitytoday.com/biblestudies/articles/spiritualformation/virtue-of-patience.html.

10 Scott Stanley, Daniel Trathen, Savanna McCain, and Milt Bryan, A Lasting Promise: The Christian Guide to Fighting for Your Marriage (San Francisco: Jossey-Bass, 2014), 18–30.

11 Willard F. Harley, His Needs, Her Needs (Grand Rapids, MI: Baker Publishing Group, 2022), 9.

12 MacArthur, 1 Corinthians, 339.

13 Paul David Tripp, Instruments in the Redeemer's Hand People in Need of Change Helping People in Need of Change (Phillipsburg, NJ: P&R Publishing Company, 2002), 90.

14 Tripp, Instruments in the Redeemer's Hand, 91.

15 Gottman, The Marriage Clinic, 35.

16 Harley, His Needs, Her Needs, 33.

17 MacArthur, Ephesians, 190.

18 Gary Smalley and John Trent, The Two Sides of Love: The Secret to Valuing Differences (Carol Stream, IL: Tyndale House, 2019), 30.

19 MacArthur, 1 Corinthians, 168.

20 Tony Evans, The Tony Evans Bible Commentary (Nashville TN: Hollman Bible Publishers, 2019), 1256.

21 Evans, Tony Evans Commentary, 1256.

22 Warren W. Wiersbe, The Wiersbe Bible Commentary: The New Testament (Colorado Springs, CO: David C. Cook, 2007), 690.

23 Evans, Tony Evans Bible Commentary, 1282.

24 Evans, Tony Evans Bible Commentary, 1171.

25 Evans, Tony Evans Bible Commentary, 1231.

26 Evans, Tony Evans Bible Commentary, 1230.

27 MacArthur, 1 Corinthians, 335.

28 Cornelius Plantinga Jr., Not the Way It's Supposed to Be: A Breviary of Sin (Grand Rapids, MI: Eerdmans, 1996), 76, 77.

29 MacArthur, 1 Corinthians, 352.

30 MacArthur, 1 Corinthians, 352.

31 John F. Walvoord and Roy B. Zuck, The Bible Knowledge Commentary (Wheaton IL: Victor Books, 1983), 535.

32 Caryl E. Rusbult and Paul A. M. Van Lange, "Interdependence, Interactions and Relationships," Annual Reviews (2003): 363.

33 Leslie Vernick, How to Act Right When Your Spouse Acts Wrong: Indispensable Guides for Godly Living (New York: Crown Publishing, 2001), 2. Kindle Edition.

34 Greg Morse, "Prophet, Priest, and King The High Calling of Christian," Desiring God (April 30, 2021), accessed March 3, 2023, https://www.desiringgod.org/articles/prophet-priest-and-king.

35 William Cutrer, Sandra L. Glahn, and Michael Sytsma, Sexual Intimacy in Marriage (Grand Rapids, MI: Kregel Publications, 2020), 71.

36 David Powlison, "How Does Scripture Change You?" Journal of Biblical Counseling 26, no. 2 (2012): 26.

A free ebook edition is available with the purchase of this book.

To claim your free ebook edition:

1. Visit MorganJamesBOGO.com
2. Sign your name CLEARLY in the space
3. Complete the form and submit a photo of the entire copyright page
4. You or your friend can download the ebook to your preferred device

A **FREE** ebook edition is available for you or a friend with the purchase of this print book.

_____

CLEARLY SIGN YOUR NAME ABOVE

Instructions to claim your free ebook edition:
1. Visit MorganJamesBOGO.com
2. Sign your name CLEARLY in the space above
3. Complete the form and submit a photo of this entire page
4. You or your friend can download the ebook to your preferred device

Print & Digital Together Forever.

Snap a photo

Free ebook

Read anywhere